THE ULTIMATE MOM

Your God Given Assignment

by

JULIE OLAMIDE ARIYO

Foreword by

OMO GHANDI-OLAOYE

The Ultimate Mom

Your God Given Assignment

by JULIE OLAMIDE ARIYO

ISBN: 978-0-9828215-1-0

Copyright© 2011 Juliana Olamide Ariyo

1st Printing 2011

Published by:
Elohiym Publishing House
11402 Clara Street
Silver Spring, MD 20902
240-375-8947
admin@elohiymhouse.com
elohiympublishing@yahoo.com

Cover Design by: Elohiym Publishing House

Printed in the United States of America

To contact the Author for speaking engagements, please write

Tel: **301-806-7112**
Email: **julieariyo@hotmail.com**

To ORDER: Please visit or call

Tel: Tel: *301-806-7112*
www.julieariyo.com
visit www.amazon.com
www.spiritselect.com

CONTENTS

DEDICATIONS

This book is a special dedication to:
The Almighty God,

My beautiful and adorable four daughters,
Adetola, Adeola, Adenike, Aderonke
For not disappointing me, and for making it easy
for me to mother them.

My four **sons-in-law for their love, faithfulness*
and words of encouragement.

*My bosom friend, who I miss dearly,
Late Mrs. Justina Oseyemi Adeyinka
Who was by every standard An Ultimate and
Unique Mom to her children

ACKNOWLEDGEMENT

The Lord Jesus Christ

*I give all the glory, honor and praise to Him for using His
mighty hands to pull me out of the fiery furnace.
Without your mercy, I would have been forgotten.
You will for ever be my Lord.*

Pastor Alex Adegboye

*I will for ever be grateful to you for leading me to Christ, and
for your spiritual guidance when it was tough; God will enlarge
your coast, and your joy shall know no bound. You are indeed a
man after God's heart.*

Pastor Ghandi & Pastor(Mrs.) Omo Olaoye

*I give a huge 'hats off' for your leadership. Thank you for
your words of encouragement, and your transparency.
Thank you for the opportunity to work with you.
You will finish well in Jesus name.*

Jesus House D.C. 'Elders Forum' & Friends:

*Special thanks to you all for believing in me. May you all live
long to enjoy the fruits of your labor.*

Yinka Agboola:

*You are a heaven sent Godson to me. Words cannot be enough to
say thank you for your prayers and support all the time. May the
hand of God be upon you and your family.*

Hon. Justice Olatunde Oluborode:
I am deeply grateful to God for making you to be my brother, confidant, and friend. Your shoulders were never tired of me at any time. You are indeed the kind of a leader that anybody will always pray to have in the family.
May your latter years be better than the former.

Mrs. Christy Oluborode:
Thank you for your motherly role in the family.

The Oluborode & Ajayi-Oromu Dynasties of Ijesha-land:
I am very proud to come from these two enviable families.

Busola Grillo
Words can not be enough for your tireless effort to proof-read this manuscript. Its only God who will repay you. Thanks a million times. You are a source of encouragement to me.

FOREWORD

This book speaks of Wisdom, Knowledge and Understanding in the art of child-rearing from a sincere Mother's point of view - in all its ramifications - and at every stage - in a contemporary world; side by side the Word of God and walk with God;

Its Contents are based on personal experiences in different seasons of life.
It cuts across cultures, ethnicity and modern values - bringing about a positive balance.

The ability of the Author to learn to abase and to abound in the circumstances that life presented, soaring high therein, succeeding and was victorious, has greatly inspired the contents of the pages of this book.

The Author has been a great student of the art that she so passionately professes and presents, having not only learnt it, but has lived it.

The Author was once a Student, but is now a Teacher; she continues to take Continuing Education LIFE - long classes in advanced level Motherhood.

She has not only learnt how best to do it; she has also learnt how not to do it; and she is generously passing it on in this book both as a Legacy and as a Testament.

Her evidence, her biological children - their lives, their values and their turnouts, are Living Testimonies of her faithfulness to the art of exemplary Motherhood per excellence.

It is a worthy Institution - a life worth living.

Have a joyous and a *"productive"* read!

(Pastor) Omo Ghandi-Olaoye
Redeemed Christian Church of God,
Jesus House,
Washington, DC

INTRODUCTION

Every woman is created to be a beautiful replica of her maker. The fact that ability to nurture is inborn in every woman makes her to be endowed with the gifts of compassion and energy to carry on her responsibility as one who provides nurture even in the face of any trial or tribulation.

As a Guidance Counselor and a mother for so many years, I am daily reminded of how a mother will one day be able to influence some other mothers in diverse positive ways to make life worth living for her and her child. It therefore calls for admiration when one sees a woman who has the gifts of wisdom, courage, strength, career excellence, nurturing a Godly child, and above all strong faith in our Lord Jesus Christ.

Concerning women, God did not create us to suffer any pain or trouble. The more we choose to recognize the devil, the more our focus is shifted. Just like the book of Psalm, **chapter 32:8** says

" I will instruct thee and teach thee in the way which thou shall go; I will guide thee with mine eye"

Each woman is to stay focused on God for direction and guidance so as to be the Ultimate Mom that God designed her to be.

Having said this, each woman is expected to shift her focus from the irrelevant things of the world, to the perseverance and tenacity of having a positive impact on the children that God has blessed her with. God is the only one who can give every woman sufficient grace to raise a child in a Godly way.

On a very serious note, of what value is a woman who has it all, but fails woefully in the area of raising a responsible and God fearing child?

It is therefore, high time for a mother who can speak the hard truth to other fellow mothers, most especially these modern day mothers, on how the act of mothering can be done without pain or stress.

Looking at the way the modern day mothers struggle to nurture their children, it is therefore the intention of the writer to provide some meaningful suggestions on how they can find the act of mothering easy, thereby, worry will be a distant memory to them.

Mothers do have a huge responsibility from God over their children. God expects every mother to build the foundation of her child's life on Him alone because any life that is built on a rugged foundation will eventually crumble. Therefore, going back to revisit the original plan of God as to how mothers are expected to raise Godly children is very crucial.

Whenever the training of a child is becoming a battle for the mother to handle, she needs a lot of wisdom,

14

and guidance from God.

A child requires a well balanced development, that is, social, emotional, spiritual, physical and psychological growth, hence a mother cannot afford to be lop-sided with her child.

The way the school time is attended to, is the same way other areas must be equally attended to. For this reason, a mother who plans to be successful needs the grace and wisdom of God for survival. Choosing to do it solely, by yourself is more or less setting yourself up for failure.

A mother's profile is expected to have positive impact on her child and on the world in general. You are to lead the way and leave a legacy that will benefit your child, his future, and the world. The most important and cherished legacy a child needs is a good training in line with God's will, such must also be a blueprint that can be opened for anyone to follow. What contribution are you planning to leave for the world to remember you by? It is only Godly principles that can bring Godly results, anything outside of this brings shame and failure.

This is why a mother's spoken words to her child must come with spiritual authority. It is contrary to the will of God for a mother to fold her hands and allow her child to wander away from God's will. On the day of judgment such a mother will have questions to answer before her maker as to how she handled what was put in her care. Without any exception, both you and your child must strive hard individually and corporately to make heaven.

Every mother is expected to be determined to win the race of motherhood at all cost. Nothing should hold you back from pursuing the goals which you set for yourself and for your children. Without you blowing your trumpet by yourself, no one else will do it well for you. It is the way you prepare your bed that you will lay on it.

Realizing that raising a child is like venturing into the unknown, except God opens ones inner eyes to see beyond the visible. Having behind my mind the importance of living a good life that is full of faith in Jesus Christ and considering honesty and integrity as equally important, helped me not to ever lose sight of my lifelong plan, and that of my children.

I decided to match on, in high spirit as a woman of courage. It was with determination and the support from God that kept me on track.

The hard determination, urged me to carve out time and all that I had, to nurture and protect my four girls to be who God destined them to be, even in the midst of thorns. Was it easy? No, but knowing Christ and trusting Him for everything at their early ages was of great help in raising them.

As a teacher for almost thirty years, praying daily for theability and wisdom to understand and succeed for all my students both in their learning and other areas of their lives was paramount to me. I teach with ease and seeing every child grow from knowing nothing to someone great at the end of each year, gives me joy and good satisfaction. It also reminds me that I am fulfilling part of what God has called me to do in life.

Knowing God, and having His merciful hands on me has definitely made the act of mothering very easy for me. He is the one who could see what others could not see. He knows that all my dependability and sufficiency are on Him, for comfort, provision, wisdom, energy, and solace. All the while, I was determined never to look back nor settle for less and by all means know that my strength keeps coming from Him.

A mother who does not have a vision or dream concerning the future of her child is living in a blind world.
Every mother is expected to dream big about what she wants for her child. It is a terrible thing for a mother to choose to take whatever comes her way for her child. I have always hated to hear people say (what will be, will be) when it comes to life in general. I want to let you know that what is supposed to be may sometimes not be, if you do not strive to work hard for it.
That is why the word of God says, in the book of *Matthew 11:12* that, it is only the violent that can take it by force. If a mother chooses to settle for just

anything when it comes to her child, this can be very disastrous.

Every mother must always pray for her children to be the head and not the tail by teaching them how to run the race of life. This must not be a lip service talk alone, but it must be backed up with action based on Godly principles. I have always had big dreams for my life and my children.

Despite all odds, I chose not to set my standards lower no matter what. Did anybody ever say it would be easy? No, but with God and determination never to look back or settle for the inferior, He brought grace to meet every need. It is impossible to reap where one does not sow.

Do you know that if you sow and you do not water, germination will be hard? Raising a child is like planting a seed, giving up along the way is just like the seed planted without watering; such a child will most likely die along the way without bearing any good fruit.

To you mothers or parents, if you abandon your child when you are meant to nurture him, you have committed a sin before God by not fulfilling your God given assignment.

Like I mentioned earlier, nurturing a child is also like running a race, if you give up in the middle of the journey, may be due to some distraction, or because the child proves to be difficult, then you have failed.

18

Unless you finish the race, you cannot claim to fulfill your God given assignment.

In as much as God has never thought of giving up on us, you can not give up on your child. Whenever you are tired and feel like giving up is the time for you to refuel for more your energy, grace and better direction from God to fight more for what you believe in. It is the duty of an ultimate mom to keep praying until something spectacular happens in the lives of her children, that is when you will be able to claim that you have ended the race well.

This book is perfect for every mother to share with her daughter. For a mother to receive a higher level of success in her mothering style as well as being a great tool in the hand of God, things must be done according to Godly principles.
You will find that as you read along, you will learn lessons from some women of strong character in the bible who not only gave birth to but raised Godly children for the kingdom of God.
Finally, the book is readable and most definite for any woman and even any man seeking wisdom and direction from God.

Becoming the Ultimate mom is very sure without any controversy, the moment every mother is willing to go back to the foundation of how God originally designed it for a mother to nurture her child.

CHAPTER

BACK TO GOD'S ORIGINAL DESIGN FOR MOTHERS.

Fellow mothers, it is high time we stop giving too much recognition to side attractions that are causing us to lose our concentration from the assignments that God gave us.

Enough is enough of the damages, and suffering in silence. We need to go back to the basic foundation of the plans of God for our lives, and step into greater positions of authority that God originally designed for us as children of the most High.

Originally, God did not create us to suffer in child birth neither did He create us to suffer dishonesty from anybody. He created us to be wonderful and beautiful in His image. Whatsoever, or whosoever took all the benefits from us must now give way, with our better knowledge of the word of God which is sharper than a two edged sword.

Fellow women, we need to rise up and go back to the foundation of our beliefs in the word of God that says we should seek God first and His kingdom, then every other thing that we need to do will come easily. We cannot continue to run after the shadow and leave our vital responsibility untouched.

Despite the incident in the Garden of Eden, God is still interested in having fellowship with us on a regularbasis. He wants us to still depend on Him for all our sufficiency.

Nowadays, every woman has one thing or the other to struggle with emotionally, socially, maritally, professionally, spiritually, and raising of children. Understanding the major role of a woman at home and in the world in general has become tougher and harder for a woman to occupy her destined rightful position.

The devil knows that if a woman's mind is pre-occupied with various challenges, it would be easier for him to penetrate and mess up the whole world. From

22

now henceforth, without any recognition to all his gimmicks, mothers must rise not to fall into his hand through the mercy of God. Just wait, as you go ahead to explore from the words of wisdom through God's inspiration from this book; pieces would be picked together, and you will be convinced that there are various ways by which you can make some crucial adjustments to take back what the devil has taken from you. It is only God's presence that guarantees a good turn around for every hope that you might have been lost.

As you make a big turn around in your life, to retrace your steps back to the original biblical principles, living a Godly life, learning from the ways some women of old in the bible nurtured their children in Godly ways, the act of mothering will be easier for both older and the modern day mothers.

God's plan for man and woman was to be comfortable in the Garden of Eden. He created Adam to cherish and love Eve. He created him to have total dominion over his environment. The devil could not comprehend why such honor would be given to a man, while he (the devil) was regarded as an outcast, hence, his hatred over the first woman was so much.

God enjoyed having fellowship with Adam and Eve on a regular basis, and they were very much connected to God. They were obeying every order given to them by God, until the devil came with his lie to make them fall flat. Despite the fact that God created the woman to listen, obey, support, and submit to the will of the man, He did not expect her to be of a negative influence on the man; Far from it. Neither did He create the man to mishandle, oppress or cheat the woman. God did not create the man or the woman to be dishonest to each other or hurt each other's feelings.

He created them to have unconditional love for each other, and to live in peace and harmony. God provided all that they would need without toiling or struggling to survive.

At the same time God set boundaries for them. He gave them order as to what they should do and what they should not do. The devil, out of his dangerous act, knew that the best way to make man fall was to go through the woman.

The devil knew that if he was able to successfully deceive a woman, it would be easy to control the man. He therefore, planned to visit the woman to lure her to break the rule set by God.

> **"God did not create woman to be a negative influence on the man.**
> **Neither did He create the man to mishandle, oppress or cheat the woman."**

With persuasion, he won the heart of the woman, and because of her influence on her husband, it helped the devil achieve his goal. The devil destroyed the good relationship

24

and fellowship between man and God. He aborted the plans of God for man and he became happy at his dangerous accomplishment.

The first woman became timid, and disappointed at her action in spite of the order given to them by God. She became helpless and unsettled for using her influence in a negative way on her husband. I could imagine how much of a regret that could have caused for her.

She must have developed some low self esteem about herself. She lost control of God given authority. Who knows? Probably, mistrust set in between her and Adam. One could imagine the kind of relationship that the consequences of her action would have brought between the two of them. Probably, the woman withdrew to herself for awhile. Fear is inevitable. What a bad devil.

They became total strangers in the environment where they used to enjoy. What they used to get easily now became unavailable, life became tough for them causing them to have to toil to get their daily meals. Bringing forth a baby became very painful and unbearable. Can you imagine the big trouble the devil put women in child bearing?

We could just have been bringing forth babies with ease, but because law and order was broken, chaos was the order of the day between the two of them. From that time, their lives were in their hands as a result of their non - compliance attitude to do the will of God. Since then, the woman lost her respect. Who knows, maybe they found it difficult to listen or pay attention to each other for sometime while apportioning of blames might have become rampant between them. Eve might have been afraid of being alone for sometime because of what the devil caused in her life. One time is enough for him to do his dangerous act. The devil had done the deed; He had broken the relationship between man and God.

He had accomplished his goal of causing confusion between husband and wife. From that time onward, the act of mistrust or doubt between husband and wife started.

Consider having children in that kind of circumstances surrounding them, what kind of training would one expect such children to get?

With an unsettled mind, a scary life that was full of hard labor for the man, no wonder, the first set of children came to life without much preparation for training.

"When God's original plan and purpose is revisited and carefully rebuilt, life will be more conducive for the mother and her offspring."

Raising them must have become a war for Eve. Cain must have been a child who wanted to do whatever he wanted to whenever he pleased. He must have been a child who would not want to lis-

26

ten to anybody's instruction, and he eventually turned out to be the first vagabond, a murderer, and even a wanderer. Since that time, the devil felt he has accomplished his mission over women without knowing the redemption plans of God for His creatures.

The devil's original mission was to keep:
* breaking the relationship between God and human beings;
* targeting every woman of destiny;
* Aborting the plan of God in the life of every gifted woman;
* Afflicting a woman with challenges to disallow her from achieving her purpose in life;
* Making a woman to suffer mistrust and dishonesty from her spouse;
* Causing a woman to break the heart of other fellow woman through greed and selfish motives.
* Making it difficult for a woman to raise Godly children.

The devil made the first woman to lose focus. He definitely knew that if he was successful in inflicting a woman with any or all of the above issues of life, it would be difficult for such a woman to settle down to think of raising a Godly child for the kingdom of God. Also, such a woman would become an emotional wreck and remain so for the rest of her life.

With this preceding knowledge, it is now time for a

27

woman who chooses to be ultimate to reclaim God's original plans and designs for her life. When God's original plan and purpose is revisited and carefully rebuilt, life will be more conducive for the mother and her offspring.

God wants to continue to have fellowship with us on a regular basis. He knows that worship and fellowship come from a peaceful mind.

Godly mother needs to go back to the foundation of God 's original design for mothering in such a way that it would be easy, fulfilling and rewarding.

It is therefore the purpose of this book to re-emphasize that every woman who plans to be unique in her duty as a Godly mother needs go to go back to the foundation of God 's original design for mothering in such a way that it would be easy, fulfilling and rewarding.

For this to be possible, it is recommended that every mother needs to go back to :

1)   Seek God and His kingdom first.
2)   Stand strong in the truth of God's word
3)   Be a praying mother
4)   Develop a strong faith in God in the raising of her child.
5)   Re-orientate her child according to biblical principles

28

6)   Be a good example of a Christian mother
7)   Re-set her priorities .

When all these are revisited, the mother will be better rooted in the word of God and Christ will be in the center of all she wants to do.

She will learn to take instructions from God on a daily basis with regards to the way to guide her child, and they will both learn to perceive issues differently, since every decision and action will be based upon the word of God.

MOTHERING IS A REWARDING PROFESSION.

I love being a woman and a mother that God has called me to be. I love everything it takes to be a woman of honor and integrity. I have found joy in the role of nurturing a child both professionally and domestically.

In fact, being in the noble and rewarding profession of a teacher continues to give me the utmost joy. Not for monetary value, but by imparting knowledge into the lives of today's doctors, engineers, architects and even God's chosen servants is something I continue to naturally enjoy. I am not like anybody, and I refuse to be less than the other. I love being a sharp, dignified, strong, warm and open minded woman. I love raising my head up high above every issue of life.

Above all, I will not trade the valuable and magnificent role that God gave me as a mother for anything; because I know and believe, more than anything that *"my payday"* shall surely come, when the reward shall begin to drop like the latter rain.

God honors any woman who fights to preserve the life of her child in the face of any danger. He honors and backs up any mother who puts her trust in Him and is able to confidently go toe to toe battle with the assurance that it will not break her down because God is on her side. He is always creating an express way in the dessert for a mother who puts herself under His umbrella for direction and protection.

There is always a reward for a mother who chooses to raise her child the way that makes God proud. The moment a mother realizes that there is time for everything, surely the season of harvest shall surely come, when she will be able to sit and relax after the long period of planting and watering.

The book of ***Ecclesiastes 3:1*** says,

> ***"To every thing there is a season,***
> ***and a time to every***
> ***purpose under the heaven"***.

Therefore, a mother needs not get tired of fulfilling one of the major assignments that God assigned to her. Every gifted and spiritual woman must be aware of what the bible says in the book of-

Ephesians 6:12
" we wrestle not against flesh and blood, but against principalities and power"

To be successful or to continue to be successful in any endeavor as a woman, one needs the leading of Christ. My fellow mothers, it is only with perseverance, tolerance, determination, consistency, truthfulness and grace of God that can make nurturing a Godly child to be easy. When a mother turns to God for strength, He equips and gives adequate direction.

Training a child is a sacred trust from the Lord.

Right now, if you have never been told, you need to get it right that to be an Ultimate mom, your job over your child can never end.

Mothering, these days is a hard work that does not get easier. It is scary, but very rewarding if successfully carried out. It starts from the conception of a child until the time the mother goes to be with her maker.

Training a child is a sacred trust from the Lord. A mother is expected to be all ears and eyes, listening and watching over her child to study his strength and

33

weakness at all time, and to assist him in getting rid of every bad character trait.

A mother who fails to seek the face of the Lord in the training of a child in a Godly way, will lose the child to the agent of the devil who is in the business of seeking who to win to his demonic kingdom.
When things go on well with a child, the mother feels accomplished, and when things take a bad turn with a child, she feels like a failure . A mother who plans to have a peaceful life at old age, must plan early in life not to fail in her duty as a Godly mother.
No wonder, the book of **Proverb 29:15b** , says,

> *" a child left undisciplined brings his mother to shame"*

This illustration simply indicates that the responsibility of child-training rests more on the shoulder of the mother. Despite the fact that the tendency for a mother's condoning disobedience from a child is higher, the above scripture gives the mother the consequence for every indulgence act allowed in the process of training.

Every responsibility of child-training rests more on the shoulder of the mother.

As a matter of fact, every career or attribute a woman possesses are only for a while. What out lives a mother are the prayers she consistently invests in the life of her child. Long after her death, the prayers will continue to work wonders in the life of that child. Prayer is the best insurance a good mother must have for her child. Whatever property or tangible item that she leaves behind is just vanity.

In sowing seeds of prayer in the life of her child, she needs to watch carefully, and be upright in the area of discipline. If you are a mother, and you have never been hated once or more by your child for setting boundaries for him, or by giving him what you feel he or she needs and not

Constantly the mother should dedicate time and days to sow seeds of prayer into the life of her child, she needs to watch carefully, and be upright in the area of discipline. She will harvest what she prayed for in prayer.

A __Mighty Harvest__ will emerge!

what he wants, then, you cannot call yourself an ultimate mom.

The ultimate mom is firm, but not strict in her way of nurturing. She believes in discipline with love, but not spoiling the child.
Motherhood is not a task that should be entered into in an ill prepared or half-hearted manner. Without mincing words, mothering should be considered the

35

most important of all professions. Even though little or no attention is given for adequate preparation for the task, the first important career a woman should pursue with her mind and might, is raising God fearing children. A mother who spends the best part of her life chasing shadows and worldly vanities is definitely jeopardizing her future by postponing her evil days, because, it is whatever she plants that she will harvest in million folds at a future date.

Looking back now, many of today's mothers realize they would have lived a better life; or even had their problems minimized if only they had mothers who nurtured them in the way of the Lord or led them to Christ early in life.

Indeed, a child whose mother has a proper under-standing of her roles as a Godly mother, and rises up to the task of raising him well, is blessed and highly favored.

Mothering is not a job for the lazy, careless, selfish, and ignorant woman. It is for the chosen, organized, and serious minded woman.

God does not promise a woman that it will be easy all through. However, as she takes the endless journey of motherhood, God's guidance will bring achievable options that will be needed for proper training of the child.

If a mother does not cultivate hope in God for guid-

ance, power, strength, direction, survival, and provision, where then shall she place her hope? Is there anything greater, more powerful, or more reliable than God?
ACTUALLY, THERE IS NONE THAT I KNOW OF.

Here is a question that rarely gets asked; Do you know that raising a successful child is a choice.? Yes it is . It depends on the way each woman perceives or defines her motherly role. As a mother, what you do not have, you cannot give, hence, mothering also can be looked at from a 'check-balance" point of view. It is wise for a mother to realize what was wrong in her youthful lifestyle, and guide against such re-occurrence as she raise her child in a better and productive manner.

God gave a mother the duty to nurture her child well, and she cannot turn her responsibility to teachers, correction officers, youth ministers, baby-sitters, and even more recently, the media through celebrities. They have their duties to perform, but, they are not to take the place of a mother. It is the mother who is to step up to the challenges and commit herself to the sacred trust given to her by

> **It is wise for a mother to realize what went wrong in her up-bringing, and guide against such re-occurrence in her child.**

God. They are ultimately not responsible for your

child's growth and well-being. A mother is not expected to give someone else her godly responsibility.

When a mother does not step up to nurture her child,
such a child becomes wild, rude, uncontrollable, and
wayward.
He roams around aimlessly like a sheep without a
shepherd. It is therefore the duty of a mother to shape
the destiny of her child.

Raising a child for the kingdom of God is
compulsory for an Ultimate Mom because it is
ordained by God just as Mary nurtured baby Jesus as
a mother, every mother must stand to exercise the
God given-authority and power over her child.
When responsibility is not carried out properly, the
devil takes over through any loophole created by the
mother.

Many suggestions or ideas in this book, are not guar-
anteed suggestions for perfect mothering, but with my
experiences of being a mother, grand mother, school
counselor and teacher for many years, I have learned
that what works for one child may not necessarily
work for the other. Above all, all suggestions put
together, with the Biblical Principles will bring good
result.

CHAPTER

'MOTHER':
A CHILD'S BEST GIFT
FROM GOD.

Yes, a mother is most definitely the best gift that a child can ever pray to have. A woman is a creature that was specially designed by God. She is the best that He saved for the last in all His creation. Concerning every mother, today I decree that the devil has failed and he will continue to fail in Jesus name. He will never succeed over our children, and our children will continue to be for signs and wonder.

A mother's duty starts from the period of pregnancy

and bringing forth a baby to life. Actually, her duty goes far beyond bringing a child into the world. Her role affects the destiny of her child. Her first emotional attachment and social interaction start when she starts to breast-feed the baby.

As from this period, she begins to learn and understand her baby's inner schedule and signals, and therefore makes accurate guesses about the child's needs and when the need arises. Staying tuned to the child's cues, picking him up and comforting him promptly, allowing him to sleep, eat, are the regular schedule of a mother. From here, a child begins to develop a basic trust in his mother as his needs are met promptly.

A mother is always strong, active and mobile. She provides comfort to her baby by rocking, walking, dancing, even without music in the middle of the night.

A mother does not sink despite any storm. Instead, she bounces back easily. She provides an interesting and conducive world for the child to explore. The first few months of a child's life takes all the attention of a mother. The mother concentrates on providing a warm, nurturing relationship and environment for the child to grow.

A mother's interaction is very important for effective learning to help a child enhance both intellectual and social skills at early age.

A mother is never tired of talking to the child even when he is unable to respond verbally. She uses the nursery rhymes to read to her child. She teaches her child some social skills and how to play through imitation.

She quickly figures out any negative play pattern and takes immediate action to correct it with love. A mother gives up her food for her child to be well fed. As a child grows up, he eats until he is satisfied, which most of the time leaves little or even nothing for the mother.

Prayer is the most effective weapon the mother uses to achieve the best concerning her child's life.

A mother's wish is to give her child her best even when it is not convenient for her. A good mother always strives to make a difference in the life of her child.

An Ultimate mother will constantly be on her knees to hear from God concerning the training of her child. Fervent prayer is a heavy responsibility upon a mother who chooses to be successful in raising a Godly child. In this regard, it is only a praying mother who can make a life-long impact on her child's life. Fervent prayer is the only insurance that a mother can

41

have to keep a child who is already doing well in that progressive direction.

For an ultimate mother, prayer is a way of life; it is her treasured joy, and her most effective weapon to achieve the best concerning her child's life. A mother who is a prayer warrior makes more progress than an uncaring, complaining and indulging mother.

It takes a determined, disciplined, and faithful mother to triumph after persistent prayer for her child to do well in life. Every woman who is determined to win the race of raising a Godly child must be willing to fight adversity in the place of prayers. In as much as our Lord Jesus Christ, who is our model knew what it was to always abide in the presence of God, there is no excuse for a woman not to do the same. He did not even take the fatherhood of God for granted, He still prayed.

A mother is the child's first teacher in life. She is her child's mirror because her child watches her and imitates whatever she does. A mother cannot only talk right, but must also make sure she walks right. She must be willing to walk in the truth of what she is teaching her child.

A Godly mother will not say, "*do what I say, and not what I do*" She must practically be a doer of whatever she teaches child. As a good mother, if you desire a

Godly child, you must take care of the foundation you set for your child. A good start will always result to a good finish. The moment the foundation for training your child is solid on Christ, it will yield a good dividend. A life that is built on the solid rock of Christ will pass the test of time.

Every instance of bad mothering can be traced to a bad foundation. God placed a great premium on child training and He does not expect a mother to joke with the way a child is trained.
The book of *Proverb 22:6* buttressed it thus;

> *"Train up a child in the way he should go, and whenhe is old he will not depart from it"*

this bible passage infers that it is what you invest in your child that you will see him bring forth. If you train him to know Christ, he will grow in it , and he will be steadfast. If you train him to be dishonest, wayward, and irresponsible, you cannot expect him to turn out to grow contrary to your guidance. It is a God given command for the mothers to train their children well, so that when they grow up they will be able to build upon the training you have given them.

If you refuse to play your motherly role as ordained by God, He will hold you accountable for destroying the life of an innocent child that is put in your custody. You have the power and authority, from God, to determine how your child turns out as an adult. From the above passage, God is saying that a mother is expected to train her child to grow up and live as a Godly adult. The instructions of a mother is very crucial in the life of a child. At the same time, a mother must have a clear vision to pursue on how to be able to give a Godly training to her child. The moment a mother realizes that training takes a lot of work, she must also understand that a child's will and attitudes are easily formed and influenced early in life, hence, a child must be taught good conduct and behaviors that are appropriate early in life so that peer pressure will not sway him or her.

Since it is a command in the bible for a child to respect and honor his parents, a child needs to be taught how to follow instructions, respect and obey early in life so that he can grow up to be a responsible adult in the home and in the community.

MAKING A DIFFERENCE IN YOUR CHILD'S LIFE :

I find it very odd to see that any woman can choose to handle the life of her child with levity. Is it possible for a woman to forget the pain of conception and bringing forth? If the answer to this is *"NO"*, I want to assume you do not need to be appealed to for you to realize your ultimate duty concerning the welfare of your child because, our unique role cannot be traded for anything.

Regardless of the manipulation of the devil, with God on your side, you must develop a high sense of responsibility and be courageous to retrace your steps to making a tremendous difference in the life of your child. You must get rid of any hindrance or limitation on your way and fasten your belt to do the job that no one else would do better for you. Once, you bring the child to the world, it becomes your sole responsibility to put your all into his welfare.

SPENDING QUALITY TIME WITH YOUR CHILD.

Many mothers feel money can do every thing but this is absolutely untrue. Don't get me wrong, money is very good, but it can't buy back any damage in a child's life. A mother who spends quality time with her child builds a good relationship with the child. Your love for your child can only be measured in the quality of time you spend with him. The joy of a mother and a child is in having a close relationship with each other. Are you the kind of a mother who is at home, but your child does not feel your impact?

You are home, and all you do is either sleep, stay on the phone, or watch every soap opera on the soap channel? Sometimes, may be when you are around in the house, it irritates you to hear the noise of your child because all your time is spent on doing some research on how to pursue or change your career. All these are good to do, but you need to realize that there is time for everything. What you need is effective time management so that, you can be better effective in all areas.

> **Avoid spending time complaining and grumbling in the presence of your child or you will feed your child's spirit with unnecessary and unneeded influence that the child too will copy as he/she grows up.**

As a mother, you can still pursue your career and play your motherly role well if you plan to manage your time very well. Are you a mother who even spends all the time nagging, complaining or imposing on your child without being objective?

Are you home and your child feels you might as well be gone?

All I am saying is for you to set your priorities right whereby you can pursue your career, and still be an effective mother. If you are a single mom, and your child shuttles between two homes due to the situation on ground, it is all well and good. God sees and knows what you are going through. He is not going to leave you nor forsake you.

You can still do your best within the framework of the prevailing circumstance. You can make your impact felt in the life of your child also. The little time he spends with you must be positively utilized. Avoid spending the time to complain or feed your child with unnecessary information. At the same time, whatever he needs to know should not be kept from him, in as much it is vital to his growth and good welfare. One day, he will grow up to know the truth.

Be careful also that you do not use the time or the opportunity to shower the child with luxurious gifts so that he or she can feel you are the best mom in the universe. Play your motherly role effectively, and let God be your advocate.

Believe me, your child needs you more than any worldly possession. He wants to understand you in totality. When you are uninvolved in child's life, you cannot expect him to be close to you. Nowadays, there are many mothers who can never be missed by their children when they are not around because there is no attachment of any kind between them. If care or attention is not paid to this area, a mother becomes a total stranger to her child and such a child goes out to seeking solace from the wrong places. No wonder, many children roam around aimlessly around in the mall, or elsewhere.

Both the mother and the child do not know anything
47

about each other , yet they live under the same roof. They are in their own separate world, doing what they choose to do. *What a horrible life!!!!*
Without pointing fingers, every woman needs to watch out and adjust before it is too late.

COMMUNICATE LOVE :

Mothers, make yourself available for your child to discuss anything and at anytime. As they grow older that bond of communication will stay intact.

God is love. God designed a family to be a replica of the love that reigns in heaven. As a mother, you must know that what your child can not get at home, he will look for it outside.

Love is everything; It is the greatest and above all other human needs.

Every child has a great need for love from his mother. Any love that is not communicated is not regarded as genuine love. The best way for you to let your child know that you love him is by allowing him to know that he is absolutely free to discuss anything with you. This assurance gives a child the confidence to know that you care.
The book of *1 Corinthians 13:13* says,

"And now these three remain; faith, hope, love, the greatest of these is love".

No matter how many gifts of the spirit one has, if one does not operate in love, all the other gifts are useless. So also a mother who does not operate in love with a child is not to be regarded as a good mother by God's standard. There is no amount of gift a mother showers on a child without communicating how much she loves the child to him, such a gift is regarded useless.

When a mother verbalizes her love, and puts it into action, she builds a great relationship with him.

Embrace Always!!!

It is good to allow a child to feel the warm embrace of the mother every now and then. It is good for a mother to give her child a hug or a pat in the back when it is needed. The touch of a hand or embrace expresses a lot of emotions that words cannot say.

The child's self confidence and esteem are built uponthis. When such a child goes out, he knows he has agood and healthy home to return to.

A child who does not feel loved at home will definitely look for a friend as a confidant. Whereas a child who is close to the mother grows up without hurting the feelings of the mother because a concrete relationship is already set.

Along with communicating love to a child verbally, it is good to allow a child to feel the warm embrace of the mother. It is good for a mother to give her child a hug or a pat in the back when it is needed. Many mothers feel embracing their children is only done when the children are young, especially among the African but this is not true. ***Embrace Always!!!***

One thing every mother needs to realize is, no matter how big or old a child is, he was once your baby, and he will continue to be forever. A pat on the back, or a kiss on the cheek is not too much to give a child to affirm your love as a mother.

MOTHER'S ATTENDANCE AT HER CHILD'S EVENTS:

It is the responsibility of a mother to find time to attend her child's special events. To some mothers, it is only the father that knows the day for every special event in the child's school. Do not get me wrong here, If this is due to some circumstances beyond the mother's control, it is ok. But it is inappropriate for a mother to make it a permanent routine.

Do you know that many mothers do not even know their children's classroom for years, not even to talk of knowing their children's teachers either personally or by name. Does this not sound absurd? Yes, it happens. *What kind of a mother are you?*

The challenges of these days require that every mother become aggressive and structured in every area of the child's life.

Many mothers feel they do not have much to contribute to their children's success because they feel doing that means rubbing shoulders with their spouses. I stand to correct such mothers that it is not true. The more your involvement in your child's life, the more the pride and confidence your spouse develops in you as a responsible woman. But, if you are the type who can not lift a finger or take any active participation concerning your child, it is not too late for you to make your impact felt in the affairs of your child's life.

You cannot be a mother whose response is always *"I don't know"*, when a question is raised concerning your child. If you show interest, you also will be a good partner in the progress of all areas of your child's life.

CHAPTER

EXTRAORDINARY MOTHERS OF OLD: *JOCHEBED, HANNA, DORCAS*

Jochebed was the mother of baby Moses. She was a Levite woman married also to Levite. She was an example of an Ultimate mom who did everything to save the life of her son. She did not give up along the way , despite the dangers she had to endure.

There was a king that was ruling in Egypt who thought the Israelites were becoming too numerous and feared that they might one day join the enemies to fight the Egyptians. He therefore, planned to oppress the existing Israelites, by ordering that every new born male child must not be allowed to exist. When the king found out that the mid-wives, out of the fear of God in their heart, were not cooperating in this regard, he ordered that every male child delivered be thrown into the River Nile.

Here comes mother Jochebed who was at that time pregnant. What do you think her prayer was? There was no ultra sound system to enable her know the sex of the baby inside her womb.

You can imagine the awful condition she would have endured through out the period of nine months. She must have been praying and fasting for the baby not to be a boy, Or probably just simply praying for the will of God .

Alas!! The baby came and he was a boy. There must have been a pandemonium in the house on that day. They must have started to run about- skelter, bringing up thousands of ideas as to what to do with the baby. Who knows, may be the mother was just planning within her mind what she could do to save her child. She must have been a praying mother who was able to seek the face of God despite the state of confusion around her.

How she came about the idea that saved her baby boy must have only been through the directives of God. This is why it is not always good to be in fear during a situation that needs immediate attention. Any decision that is taking in fear is not always the best, but one taken in the place of prayer and communing with God.

Jochebed hid her son for three months. From this action, one would think , that Jochebed sensed something special about the life of her son, hence she could not afford to lose him. Did the baby cry? Yes, but God kept him, He looked at the heart desire of the mother. He saw the secret tears of the mother. I am sure the mother would have been crying louder than the baby so that people passing by would not notice that there was a new born in the house.

> **She seemed to be a woman who would persistently wait for God to give her directives on what to do to save her baby**

She must have been a woman who would have been persistently waiting for God to give her directives on what to do further to save the baby. Her story is expected to be of great inspiration to every mother. I am sure if she had sought help or advice from friends or neighbors, she would been misled. Probably, they suggested that she threw the boy into the Nile to preserve her own life or they might have gossiped about her and put her into trouble. I hope all mothers can learn a big lesson from this story, that , there is time to speak, and there is time to be quiet. It must have been in the secret place of God that she chose to hide the boy that God dropped the idea of the papyrus basket in her heart.

Actually, the dimension and everything about the design of the basket must have come through the leading of the holy spirit. She made it to be watertight, and then she put the baby into it and laid the basket by the brink of the river Nile where the queen used to bath. She did not just put her child there and forget about him. She followed the basket.

A mother who does not have the holy spirit must have wandered away out of fear, this woman kept the sister of the baby to hide from a distance to watch over the boy from afar off.

I wonder what Jochebed herself must have been doing at that point in time. She must have been praying to God to perform His usual miracle for the boy. God who had known the end of the baby right from his birth, performed His wonders again, by sending the queen of Egypt out to the river. Hearing the cry of the baby, she looked and was overwhelmed with pity, for she knew it was an Hebrew child.

If the mother did not put Miriam at a distant to watch the baby from far, no one could have known the whereabout of the baby. The mother eventually was the one who took care of the baby while God favored her by getting paid honorably. He was named Moses by the queen of Egypt.

All these happened because Jochebed was a mother who was spiritually sensitive. She decided not to be of the world at that time, but to hold on to God who gave her a baby boy, despite, King Pharaoh's decision. She believed that God would do something miraculous concerning her situation.

Fellow mothers, if it were any of us, would you have been able to go thus far for a child? Would you be able to keep the baby for one night, not to talk of three months? This is a big lesson for us all. All of us are called to raise children for the kingdom of God. Jochebed raised a man who later became the deliverer of Israel.

Mothers, you do not know what your child would turn out to be tomorrow. Do your best with the leading of God, do not go ahead of God, but rather let Him go ahead and you follow. Going ahead of Him leads to disaster. Jochebed held to her son even in the face of death, she kept looking unto God who intentionally gave her a baby boy at the time that was really tight to take care of him. She eventually passed the test of time.

Jochebed continues to remain a perfect example of an Ultimate mom. She was a living example of a Godly mother; she prepared Moses for the palace. She recognized that Moses had a destiny to fulfill, and she did not allow distraction to tamper with his destiny In fact, she was a good example of a mother did not mind to die for the life of her son. What a courageous and Godly mother who refused to give up despite all odds.

HANNAH

There was a man from the country of Ephraim who had two wives by name Peninnah and Hannah. The name of the man was called Elkanah. Peninnah had many children while Hannah had none, but Elkanah loved Hannah more than the other woman.

Whenever they had to go for their yearly worship in Shiloh, the husband normally gave double portion to Hannah for her own sacrifice , while the other woman would be given according to the number of children she got.

Hannah was barren and her mate always made fun of her, nevertheless, her husband loved her so much that he thought he could take the place of a son in her life The husband once met her crying, and consoled her by telling her that he was more than ten sons to her. Though, the statement was an indication of a genuine love for her, but it did not compare to the motherly love that she was yearning to give if she could have her own children. Elkanah's statement to Hannah was very deep; It showed the heart of the man towards Hannah, but I do not know how a man's love could be more than ten sons for a woman.

I want to believe that the man meant everything he

was telling Hannah, but there were two women in the house. Who knows, Hannah might be under pressure not only from Peninnah , but also from the family members. Lets face the reality, it could have been that when Hannah appeared at any family function, Peninnah and the family members would giggle by saying, *"Here comes, the husband's heart"* and other forms of horrible jests. Hannah must have been receiving awful statements that would have been given persistent broken heart.

The more the man kept reassuring her of his love, the more her sadness probably was rekindled. What a life! Regardless of any situation, Hannah's husband still had some children from his other wife who gave him joy.

Having two women under the same roof could have been humiliating to Hannah, more so, there was no child to cheer her up in her own small world. The pressure from the right, left, and center probably made Hannah to realize she needed to do something about her situation.

Thank God, she did not take a bad decision. She could have thought of giving it back to her Peninnah, which could have her to lose her concentration about reminding God.

Hannah chose to concentrate and face her battle squarely in the place of prayer. She must have realized that the best of men will continue to be a man. She realized that her solution was in the hands of God alone, so she placed all her trust in Him.

Instead of relying on the continuous affirmation of love from her husband, Hannah took the battle to God where it would be carefully targeted.

When they went to Shiloh for the yearly worship, she prayed desperately with a vow and God looked down on her from heaven and answered her prayer.

Hannah became a mother the following year, and she named the baby Samuel, because she asked of him from God.

Mothers face your battles concerning your children squarely for the best of men will still always be a "man". All solutions are in the hand of God

Samuel grew up, and the mother took him to the house of God in Shiloh according to the vow she made with God. Samuel grew to be a great priest in Israel. He ministered before the Lord under Eli. Samuel grew up to be loved by God, the Lord was with Samuel as he grew up, and the Israelites recognized that Samuel was a prophet of God.

From this, it could be seen that Hannah's trust in God made a way for her. Thank God for using Peninnah to push Hannah to her destiny. If Peninnah did not provoke her, she might not be moved to seek God the way she did. Sometimes in life, we need somebody to push us to get out of our comfort zone to do the right thing. Whatever the enemy planned for evil is at times what God will use to bring us His good.

As a result of the intimidations and pressures from everywhere , Hannah made a good choice to cry unto the Lord who was able to wipe her secret tears. She knew that it was only God who could do what no man could do because if it was within the power of her husband to have a child, she would have gotten as many children as she wanted.

In the end, God did not just give her a child, but a child that one could be proud of . Samuel alone was more than ten sons for Hannah. After she released Samuel unto the Lord. God honored her for fulfilling her promise and she had more children who gave her more joy after Samuel.

Every mother should learn to depend on God alone for any and everything. He is the only one whose gift is permanent. Valuable time should not be wasted on any distractive things, instead, one should stay focus to be able to pray to God for her need. Thank God that Hannah did not spend her whole life giving it back to the mate, she used all her insults as raw materials to take her to where her destiny was.

God remembered Hannah and He wiped her secret tears away. He gave her double for her portion, because a son l ike Samuel is a child in a million. A woman like Hannah could have forgotten the vows she made with God when life became comfortable for her. She could have decided to keep Samuel to her heart, and planned to strike a deal with God, by telling Him,

" God, you know , by the time you give me another child, I would be able to fulfill the promise, because I want people who knew me as a barren woman see me with this child. People need to know that I am now a mother". Or, she could have said , "how would people know that I had a child like them"?

Hannah did not do this. She did not waste her time on any public opinion. This behavior showed that she was in the world, but not of the world. She did not care if people would feel she did not yet have a child. She strongly believed in the fact that by giving Samuel away, God would still do the same miracle again. It was her strong faith in God that opened her womb for more children.

The bible did not record the names of the other children by the other woman, however, it was Samuel who came after a long wait that made the name of the father to be heard.

The fact that some people start earlier does not mean that they will be better than those who start late. Whoever starts earlier is not going to stop you from getting to the same place.

Samuel came to life at his own appointed time and he was highly celebrated. Samuel did every thing he did in Israel according to the leading of God because he had been hearing God right from his youth.

Mothers, would you mind if I decide to cut it deeper again? Can we look at the character of Peninnah in the house in totality? Are you like that to your fellow friends or relatives, or any other person? I know many might take this personal, without being judgmental, lets be real and call a spade a spade; You are not God. He is the only one who has the last say about any situation.

Why do you want to switch the role? God gives when He likes and takes when He likes. By the character of

There is a plan and time for every child God created. Waiting long to have a child means to expect a child of special honor.

Peninnah, she thought all hope was gone concerning Hannah. She thought she had it all. She might even have planning to inherit all that Elkannah had, since Hannah was barren.

She might have been planning to grab or accumulate as much as she could for her children.
Do you know that this kind of a woman might not even have time to pray for her own children?
All her concentration might have been on how Hannah would be frustrated out of the home. What a woman? This is why the bible says that the heart of man is desperately wicked, who can know it. What is

in your mind concerning another person? Check your minds and make amends.

Go back to the basic of your foundation in Christ and seek Him with your heart . Make amends where necessary and live a holy life. Let God be the architect of your life. God's thoughts are not our thoughts.

The very place where man feels it is ending is where God is starting. Remember, whatever you sow is exactly what you are going to reap. Everybody has her own appointed time and season with God. Another lesson that every mother should learn from the life of Hannah is power to endure and to tolerate in the midst of storm. She stayed focus even in the midst of all the provocation, pressure, intimidation from the mate and family members. Instead of her allowing the problems to break her, it built her up to stay in place of prayers.

It was the trust and faith she had in God that enabled her to make the kind of vow she made. Ladies, I want you to hold on to the fact that whatever God does not give you , it means you do not need it.

If you are facing any kind of persecution, you must believe that God is not ignorant about it. At His own time, He will show forth.

If you desire a child like Samuel, it is high time you learn to believe what God says about your life; do not act on the lie of the devil; and above all try to prophesy the word of God into the life of your children and surely, your expectations shall not be cut off.

DORCAS

In Joppa, there was a woman named Dorcas, meaning Tabitha. She was seriously sick, and she eventually died. Her death made everybody who knew her to be sad, to the extent that they gathered to look for the man of God to come over and pray to God concerning Dorcas. All the widows surrounded the body of Dorcas to mourn and wait for the arrival of Peter.

Peter left Lydda where he just performed a miracle of healing to go to Joppa where everybody was waiting for him to perform a miracle on Dorcas. Upon his arrival, he requested that all the widows who were weeping as they surrounded the body of Dorcas to step outside. Peter got down on his knees and prayed. He then turned towards the dead woman, and said,

'Tabitha, get up ".

Immediately, Dorcas opened her eyes, and sat up. Peter took her by the hand and helped her out. This could only be God. Dorcas came back to life in good condition of health.

The bible recorded it that while Peter came inside the room where the dead woman was laid, the widows showed him all the robes and clothes that Dorcas made for them while she was alive. It was also recorded that she was always doing good while she was alive.

It was the act of her giving and love to people that moved everybody to be desperate on doing something to bring Dorcas back to life. This was the effect of good character.

What will people say about you when you are gone? Have you ever thought about this? Are you the kind of a person who enjoys causing people to pain and sadness so you can get to the top? Do you enjoy oppressing people with what you have? Did you detach other people's roof to cover your own head ? You need to think of when you will no longer be able to defend yourself.

Though, many people do not really care about what happens after they are gone; If you are truly a child of God, and you believe in the resurrection power of our Lord Jesus Christ, you will learn a big lesson from this woman's life history.

Another lesson we need to learn from this story is that it is only God who has the last say about the calendar of ones life. It can never be over, until God says it is over. I believe God had more assignments for the woman, to complete which is why God raised her from the dead back to life.

Dorcas was a unique woman by every standard of life.

CHAPTER

OVERCOMING THE BATTLES OF MOTHERHOOD

This chapter goes into details with examples and traits
that every mother should know and understand; working towards this traits to be able to win the battle and
challenges of being a mother.

Training a child means putting your time, your love
and energy into teaching acceptable behavior according to biblical principles. You are expected to let your
focus and perseverance have great impact in the life
of your child. God's word has already given you the

practical way of mothering a Godly child;

Proverbs 22:6 says

> ***"Train up a child in the way he would go,***
> ***when he grows up , he will not depart from it".***

If this is followed correctly, both you and your child will live longer and happier in life.

First and foremost, as a mother you need to allow your child to know that your total dependency is on God. Try to be real with your child. The more you pray and fellowship with your child, the deeper the word and fear of God will be rooted in him. Also sharing your heartfelt thoughts and feelings together will be easy.

Allow your child to understand the realities of life, and allow him to know that you are not the most perfect person on earth. Do not claim to know it all, be honest with your child as this will make him/her develop confidence in you. It will also build trust as your child grows, and he or she will always trust your opinion   concerning any issue.

To win the battle of mothering:

(1)   **A MOTHER SHOULD TEACH HER CHILD THE WAY OF THE LORD.**

It is the duty of a mother to start early to teach her child the way of the Lord. The easy way to introduce Christ to a younger child is by letting him know how Christ loves everybody including his family. Tell the child how God will bring healing in times of sickness, provision at every need so the family does not lack; this will help your child to be inquisitive about who God is.

Tell him that when-ever he sleeps, God sends His angels to watch over him at night. Narrate the story of how Jesus was born as a baby and grew up just like him too, this helps

> **Gradually, and consistently teach your child the simple way of praying in a brief and simple manner.**

create a familiarity with the word of God. As you go on like this in a simple way, you will see the curiosity to want to learn more.

If you make your introduction to be very ambiguous and very abstract, your child will lose interest. Gradually, start to teach your child the simple way of praying in a brief and simple manner.

As a teacher, I prefer to teach my pre - kindergarten pupils to learn to pray like this, *"Thank you for my mummy, thank you for my daddy, thank you for my teacher, and thank you for my family, in Jesus name I pray."* When it is time for lunch, we pray like this, *'Thank you God for my lunch, in Jesus name I pray.'* At that age, that is the simple way by which the chil-dren can learn how to pray. Long prayers will be complicated and meaningless to them, so let your child understand that praying is talking to God, who is our father in heaven. Tell him that God is every where we are, and He listens at all times even though, we cannot see Him, but He sees us. All this step by step teaching will make God to be real to your child as he grows up. To crown it all, gradually try to narrate the story about the growth of Jesus to him, tell him or her how Jesus grew up to be a little boy who was always listening and obeying his parents.

You can also tell him about the growth of various characters in the bible like Samuel and Joseph. Try to read the bible to him/her both day and night. It is better you start with a children's bible that has beautiful pictures of people you discussed.

Before you know it, your child will grow to know and trust God. As you have made it easy for your child to pray, he will develop in it

Step by step approach to biblical knowledge will be retained by your child with proof of it in adulthood.

and continue to grow and increase in the knowledge of God.

Whenever you as a family are now doing the family devotion together, the more interesting the devotion will be and the more your child will be looking forward to it. Learn to use examples that are real, if possible the ones your child can see or know about.

Agree on some prayer points and see how God will work wonders to prove Himself real to your child. You can then further teach him how to have his own quiet time. As he grows up in age, teaching him the step by step way of praying will be easier for both of you to embrace.

Let them understand the importance of praise and thanksgiving to God at the beginning of every prayer. Teach him that he needs to cleanse himself from all the committed sins, and never go back to such sins any more.

Go further to let him know that he can present his requests unto God through the name of Jesus. Help him realize that God is every where, hence, he can communicate with God anywhere and anytime. As your child increases in age, his level of understanding the word of God will also increase. You should go ahead to help him develop his spiritual growth by allowing him to lead prayer sessions and practice to read and share the word at his own level of understanding. You will be surprised to see the way your child will begin to grow. Leading your child to Christ must not be enforced, but rather, done with a gradual process. The more you teach him about Jesus and His miraculous work, sharing testimonies as a family will further convince him.

71

THE ULTIMATE MOM; Your God Given Assignment

It is your duty to let him know that he needs to develop a personal relationship with God. Let him know that constant meditation on the word is crucial. Try not to be the kind of a mother who leaves her child home while going to church. Make sure that your church has a vibrant children's church where your child can learn the word of God.

Be a living example for your child. You are the book your child reads
You must practice what you teach him.
Your own faith will be tested by your child before he/she can believe the truth.

It is your duty to always cross check and discuss the lesson learned from the church with your child on regular basis. This will allow you to know the level of his spiritual growth.

Learn to share stories of Godly children from the bible and also those who did not follow the ways of the Lord. Let him learn the consequences of every behavior. Let your child learn about the bad behavior of the two sons of Priest Eli and the consequences of such behavior over the household of Eli. Finally, you must be a living example for your child. You must practice what you teach him. Your own faith will be tested by your child before he can be able to believe you. If you are the kind of a mother that gets scared at a little occurrence that is not palatable, you cannot teach your child about faith. You must

72

learn to practice what you teach him. Teaching him to trust God will make him grow to stand firm in the midst of any storm. Sharing of testimonies with your child will boost his spiritual growth and faith. Give him time to ask any question from you and learn to answer each question without condemnation.

(2)   A MOTHER SHOULD NOT BE AN AUTHORITATIVE PERSON:

You cannot use the standards of this world to handle your child. Though the scripture authorizes you to be in authority over your child, however, you need to exercise the authority with love and fairness. You need to understand that it is God who owns the child, not you.

God gave him to you to guide, so you are to have your authority over him according to Godly principles . Do not get me wrong, being authoritarian does not make you to be a bad mother, but being too strict will not bring any good result. You have the right to discipline your child if he misbehaves, but it has to be done in love.

Giving your child some freedom is not supposed to give him room to be indulged in any behavior that disrespect you or others. Too much freedom is why some mothers do not have any clue about who their children are.

Giving your child some freedom should not allow the

73

child to talk back to you . Mothers who are fifty years and above grew up under a different situation in which they just had to obey any rules set by their parents.

In those days, there was nothing like democracy in the family. Our mothers chose our clothes, approved of our friends and even schools and career to pursue without any question. Mothers even had authority over who their children should marry. Growing up, with an authoritarian father, nobody in the family dared say no to his orders. We had to do whatever he told us.

We learned in a hard way. Though, the system was very harsh and tough, but it worked for many people in my generation because, we did not have an alternative idea of how life should be other than to obey. Actually, a child had no choice other than to succeed in his endeavors because his parents put a very high premium on their names.

Now, times have changed. Being a child nowadays is totally different because, many mothers struggle with setting boundaries for their children. You can show love to your child and still set your rules. At the same time, if you are too harsh with your child nowadays, you will lose him. It is when he is free to tell you anything, that life will be comfortable for both of you. Children need to think independently and the

74

ability to express themselves nowadays.

Our generation of mothers back then, were not given any opportunity to express ourselves, but thank God for those who had understanding parents. An attempt to want to control every aspect of your child's life nowadays will make him keep you at an arms length. Children no longer want to be viewed as inferior, they like to voice their opinion out.

A mother who does not want to lose her

A mother will learn to listen and reason with her child as the need arises.

A child's opinion must not be totally discarded.

child to the world, will not be too strict nowadays. She will learn to listen and reason with her child as the need arises.

She will not claim to always be right. She will be will-ing to welcome criticism from her child sometimes, because out of this, they will agree to disagree and vice versa.

A child's opinion must not be totally discarded. A child who is not allowed to think by himself will develop the spirit of resentment against anybody that comes his way. A mother is not suppose to do all the thinking for her child. Your child too needs a lot of growing to do , so that he does not feel suffocated and act silly in public. He needs to be prepared for the real world.

It is so ironic how some parents treat their children in a very awkward manner, such parents refuse to appreciate the children God gave them. Instead of nurturing them in love, they ignore or abandon them for no good reason or for reasons which they believe is justified.

What kind of example is such a parent portraying to the child? What will such a parent give as an account to God on the assignment of nurturing placed in his hands? God will not bend His rules because of us. It is about time that such a parent repent. When you do not treat your child with the fear of God in your heart, you will be sinning against God who puts you in charge to nurture the child.

The bottom line is, such a child needs to play his role as a Godly child according to the biblical principles by not exhibiting any negative reaction despite the kind of treatment he receives from the parent. It is very important for every mother to realize that excessive authoritative rule do more damage than good in the lives of children. Raising your child according to God's principles is the key thing.

It does not make you less of a mother. God wants you to mother your child the way He parents us with firmness and love. At the same time, He does not want you to choke him with a selfish kind of love.

Godly principles will always bring Godly results. A mother who wants the best for her child must learn to discipline the child according to the word of God. Though discipline seems to be difficult to teach a child, it is the best way to let a child know that there are boundaries that he cannot exceed. A child who accepts biblical discipline grows up to succeed in life. He grows up to have good character, respect for God and for every other human being therefore, correct your child with love. Give him various Godly opportunities to choose from and by this , he will learn to make good decisions for himself. Teach him the realities of life, let him know that life is not always going to be a bed of roses, and that everyday cannot always be a Christmas day.

Teach him to know that there is time for plenty, and there is time for scarcity in the life of every human being. Teach him how to plan for the rainy day in his life.
Learn to teach your child to grow up to be a mature adult, who will be ready to face the struggles of life and come out successfully.

Learn to train your child to be able to stand tall with his head up high, and to be able to think for herself; this will build her self esteem.

Having said all this, mothers are not forbidden to take a good action to discipline a child who misbehaves. The bible gives room for correcting your child and guiding him rather just spanking alone.

When you discipline your child in love, not too authoritatively or too permissively you will get good result.

There is a place for corporal punishment from a mother, but I believe too many mothers use it when they don't have to. Many mothers even believe the only language their children understand is spanking. This does not always stop bad behavior because if it really works, I do not think it would be necessary to warn a child from doing a bad thing more than once. Sometimes, constant spanking makes a child grow wild, and makes him not to take you seriously anymore.

You are to bring him up your child with the loving discipline that the Lord approves. In the process of wanting your child to behave well, do not make your child look silly.

Many children find it difficult to voice out any opinion in the presence of their mothers, because of the fear of getting into trouble.

I want to encourage mothers to discipline their children in love. Allow your discipline to start from home. Actually, discipline should be seen as a way of correcting a child in love.

A child who is corrected in an authoritative way tends to become a rebellious child, who will one day be looking for a way to retaliate. Such a child pretends to be a good child in the home but as soon as he has the opportunity of stepping out of the home he starts to rebel.

Sometimes, such a child refuses to accept the faith. Though, the home environment is the best place for your child to study lifelong experience, it is also in the home that he can learn to be loved and to be corrected.

A mother's emphasis should be far from the controlling attitude, but rather teaching the child with the kind of love that Christ has for us. The mother who has the understanding that God is in authority over her, will understand how to exercise her own God given authority over her child.

It is high time we mothers stop the notion that if a child is not controlled, he will get out of hand, and that he will go in the wrong direction. I am not saying that a child should be allowed to let loose, or not guided, or be neglected.

What I am saying is that, mothers must know that each child is unique, no two children are the same, hence each child needs a different approach or method of training. When you discipline your child in love, not too authoritatively or too permissively you will get good result. You should maintain a good relationship with your children.

The relationship should be a healthy one , free from a selfish motive. The relationship must be God based with biblical principles.

A mother should allow her teaching to be based on reality. A mother should maintain consistency, not blowing cold and hot at the same time. She should teach her child to respect himself and others. You should teach the child to grow from being a child to an adult. The kind of teaching you give your child will determine his closeness to you.

A child who is under the control of an authoritarian mother will be afraid of telling the truth about anything to the mother since he knows that telling the truth about any bad behavior to his mother will definitely cause trouble, he will prefer to lie so he can please her. Such a child would prefer to lie in order to gain the love of the mother. The only way to discourage this attitude is for you as a mother to let your child know how bad it is to tell lies. Let him know that God does hate liars. Trusting more will prevent him from lying to you.

Above all, do not compare your child with any other child. He is a unique child, created differently for God's purpose. This is why no two thumb prints can ever be the same. When your training is based on love, mothering will not be as difficult as we feel. Let me be frank with you; giving your child some freedom, does not mean that you are allowing him to have his way or that you are giving him undue advantage. Learn to give him the chance to grow to be an adult who can stand and pass the test of time.

The closer you are to your child, the more you will know when he needs to be curbed or encouraged in certain behaviors. The more you learn to allow your child to express himself before you, the more chance you get to straighten him up, if he is on the wrong track. Keeping a child quiet makes him keep to himself, and such allows him to exhibit all the behavior which he was unable to show at home when he gets outside of the home.

(3)　A MOTHER SHOULD NOT BE OVER PROTECTIVE .

A mother is expected to toughen up her child, so that he can be ready to cope in the real world. She is to let the child know that life is hard, and he should be ready to face it. She should tighten the belt of truthfulness around him, so that his life does not fall apart.

Dress him/her for the battle of life, so that he can stand victoriously at the end and give the glory to God for having someone like you as mother all the days of his/her life.

81

Love is not giving your child everything he wants but what he needs. It is inappropriate for a mother to let a child have whatever he wants and do whatever he wants to do. Doing this depicts that there is no orderliness for the child. An expression of your love to your child is not supposed to make you become the child. You are not expected to switch your role with your child. God has made you to be the mother, and you should not because of the love you have for your child forget your God given assignment over him.

You are supposed to place your priority only on him and on nothing else even he is your only child. It is not to make you do what he can do by himself for him. A mother who does all these is not expressing love, but rather spoiling the child. Such a mother is over protecting the child and not allowing him to grow and mature.

Many mothers destroy their children with too much attention. You are not expected to do for him what he is capable of doing for himself. Many mothers even go to the extent of doing their children's homework for them making the children to live in a fool's paradise. I mean things like writing the homework for their children.

Such mothers will intentionally miss some of the questions, so that the teacher will feel the children did it. Who is the teacher grading? Is it the mom or the child? Who is deceiving who? A mother who does this constantly is the one who is expected to receive a diploma and not the child when the child is done in the school. Upon graduation, will she attend job interviews with the child? If you are that kind of a mother, you need to change your parenting style and let your child grow.

Allowing him to know that he is the one in school and not you is absolutely important. You need to know that you will not be there for him forever. I am not saying that mothers should not help their children with their homework, but you are not to do it for them. Your own is to guide them, probably help read and explain the instructions to them. Help to build them up, and not destroy them because you want them to be in the good book of the teacher so they can win all the awards, that you know they don't deserve. This will teach your children to be honest and accountable.

When you over protect your child, you are making him believe that he cannot do anything on his own. Such a child will lack initiatives and exposure. Such a child will not know what freedom is and will always want to cling to you forever. God does not want you to burn yourself out. He wants you to have peace, and to have it abundantly.

Allow your child to have more responsibility and some freedom in life. A child who is being over protected, will not know how to think on his own, because he is regarded as the centerpiece of the home. When such a child is given the opportunity to step out of the home, may be to a College outside the home, there comes the big problem. Such a child will misuse the freedom because he will not be able to handle it. He might end up falling into the wrong group of friends or start to drink, smoke, etc. Sometimes, such a child may even backslide from the Godly foundation that may have been set for him.

(4) A MOTHER SHOULD NOT BE IMPOSSIBLE TO PLEASE.

Are you the kind of a mother who can never be pleased with anything? Are your standards too high to meet? Are your expectations too high for your child.? Or may be your standards, are set based on your friend's child's performance without any consideration on your child's uniqueness. Instead of you calming down to realize that you cannot use your parent's yardstick to measure the way you are to raise your own child, you are busy using all the olden days method in this century which will make your child to be miserable.

If you are the kind who finds fault in everything your child does, the two of you cannot have any good relationship.

Act of perfectionism will not make you to know the true character of your child. The moment he knows that you are not easy to please, he will pretend to satisfy you, but as he leaves home, he will change. If you are a mother who is always looking for fault in whatever your child does, you will always end up doing what your child can do by yourself because you are never satisfied until you do it yourself.

You cannot overlook any spot on your cooker, books on the shelf must be properly fixed in a particular way. A few crumbs on the kitchen counter can almost make you tear the house down, you are just wearing yourself out with insignificant things. This kind of behavior has a lot negative effect on you and your child. Before you know it, you are stressing yourself and you are gradually sending your child out to look for comfort elsewhere, because he already knows you to be a mother who can never be satisfied. What a name.

Do not be a mother who can never be satisfied.
Its dangerous !

If you are this kind of a mother, let me tell you that your child will have a sense of inadequacy and he will even become a lazy person because you prefer to do all your stuff by yourself rather than allowing him to learn on the activity. Your child will develop negative thoughts that will yield negative actions. He will assume that he is not good enough for you, since you are never satisfied with his performance.In his attempt to please you, he will decide to be silent. He may be fed up of you and just decide to ignore you. What a great insult on your part as a *" too- know mother"*.

You need to calm down, and learn to appreciate other people. Avoid running people around you or even your child crazy. The fact that you were raised that way does not mean your child will enjoy such perfectionism.

It is very good to be organized, and be very neat, but do everything with moderation so as not to lose your child. Show him the easy way of getting things done. Even if it is not as perfect as you expected, learn to appreciate him so that he can keep improving. Empowering him with praises helps to develop his self esteem.

The more you practice this habit regularly, you too will be able to release tension and there will be joy and happiness around you and in your home. Learn to show enthusiasm about his accomplishment. The less your complain, the more your child will grow up to be emotionally stable. Being tolerant and accommodative to your child does not mean that you are not firm, neither does it mean that you are an indulging mother.

Above all , take life easy, be more receptive, learn to enjoy the company of your child and people around you, because you only have one life to live.

There is still room to change to enjoy the remaining part of your life with people around you most especially your children and future grandchildren. You need to let your existence count in a positive way. I pray that the holy spirit will be welcomed and allowed to be the one to guide and lead every mother in nurturing her child in a Godly way without being stressed.

(5) A MOTHER SHOULD EMPATHIZE WITH HER CHILD.

Showing of empathy by a mother towards her child, brings peace, joy and understanding in the home. This will be more explained upon when we talk about your teenage children.

Let your child understand that he/she is in charge of the choices he/she makes in life by how matters are handled.

Learn to put yourself in the position of your child whenever he tries to discuss with you before you jump into conclusion.

The moment you realize that it is not everything a child says that does not make sense, you will take time to think deep, before any feedback. When both of you have a positive attitude towards an issue, both of you will be able to come to logical and reasonable conclusion which will not be one sided.

If there is a need for you to say "NO" to a particular activity that your child wants to do, let him know your reasons for going against his plans and endeavors. Help him to throw more light into such discussion. Give him a different scenario about life experiences that may be of help to him in his decision making. Let him know that you are after his interest and not after any selfish motive.

Finally, conclude your discussions with letting him understand that he is in charge of any choice he makes, so also the consequence. By doing this, he will remember in future should he be faced with a similar situation.

(6) A MOTHER SHOULD BE AN ENCOURAGER:

Encouragement brings improvement, and gives a child high sense of responsibility. If your child makes a mistake, do not abandon him or make any negative and demoralizing comments.

Instead, you need to let him know that mistakes and failures are meant to build someone up to be able to perform better in future. Always stress the positive to him. Show him that you love him despite the failure. Let him know that if he falls, he will definitely rise again.

This is the time that he needs your cooperation more

than anything to be able to rise above the ugly mistake.

If you fight him, or discourage him, you will throw him out for the devil to attack.

The most wayward child needs the love and encouragement of a mother to bring him back home to his sense. It was because the prodigal child knew that he would be welcomed back home by his father that gave him the courage to change his mind to go back home.

The moment you realize the fact that no mother will exchange her own good child for your bad one, you will think twice before you decide to write off your child. Whatever child you have, you better cherish him and mold him to a better child. Do not get me wrong, I am not telling you to succumb to a bad behavior from a child. What I am saying is that you should practice unconditional love with your child, and do not compare him with anybody's child.

This does not mean that you should not discipline him whenever he deserves to but, let your discipline be a reality one. The kind that is done with love, patience, and understanding, and that, if he refuses to show respect , you are not necessarily going to succumb to his idea.

You should try to understand that children have different lifestyles and values. Avoid criticizing them negatively. If your child knows that you have his interest in mind, he will learn to respect you. Sharing your feelings with your child makes him see you as a mother he can trust and relate with.

(7) A MOTHER SHOULD NOT OVER-PAMPER HER CHILD.

The Scripture that says *"Train your child the way he should go ...."* does not say you should pamper your child, so that when he grows up, he will cherish you for being a good mother.

Fellow mothers, looking back into the history of men and women who are great today, it will be difficult to find one who would give a testimony of ever been pampered or indulged by his or her mother. It is duty of a wise mother to know the difference between spoiling a child and loving him. It is very rare to see a spoilt child do well in life. Pampering a child, does not increase the beauty or the intelligence of a child, instead it destroys his future. Having a child at an old age does not mean that the child should be spoilt. A wise mother quickly rises up to the discipline of her child early in life.

A spoilt child will bring shame and dishonor of the mother.

A spoilt child cannot stand any challenge of life. The child feels everything should be done for him since he is used to getting everything he wants very easily. He does not think of the future, because the mother does the thinking and planning for him. He is not used to struggling to achieve anything, and neither does he know how to compete for anything.

He is contended with whatever he is giving whether good or bad. He does not work towards building himself, but rather, he is open to being cheated by mates or even younger ones. He looks for attention anywhere he is and feels the whole world is centered around him.

He does anything he wants without any remorse. A spoilt child has a higher tendency of bringing shame to the mother at the end of the day.

Samuel was never spoilt by mother Hannah. If Hannah were to have pampered Samuel, she should not have released him to Eli. She should have kept him in the house to show Peninnah that she too had a child.

Look at what Samuel turned out to be in Israel. The shame and damage Eli's children brought to the life of their father was without any measure. His neglect and indulgence on his two children brought calamity upon him and the children. Who knows, may be, his two sons were in charge of everything in the home, while Samuel would be sent on various errands for them. Hannah never had to suffer any sleepless night about what was going on with Samuel in Eli's house. Over pampering a child brings damage to his life. I know that many mothers would have probably been saying , " It is because you are not in my position, that is why you refuse to understand how difficult it is to have only one child".

Let me tell you, there is a way you can show your love to your only child without spoiling him. There is a way you can train your child without destroying his future.

Hebrews 12:10-11 says,

" For they verily for a few days chastened us after their own pleasure; But he for our profit, that we might be partakers of his holiness".

You are to correct your child with Godly love, not with a rotten love, that will not allow him to think by himself, nor do anything by himself. You must be firm with your child and give him loving correction.

> **A form of recognizable form of punishment and standard will bring consistency in discipline**

Avoid overlooking every little detail in the life of your child, and try to stop every undesirable habit that you notice with your child as you notice it, don't wait.

Sometimes, a child who is young can be called to order, with a simple 'time out'. This is to let him know that he is getting out of boundaries and that he needs to stop.

For an older child, allow him to understand that every behavior or choice has its consequence. Try to set reasonable standards for a child to follow, and as you do this try to consider the age of the child in question. Make sure your standards are not too high or too low for him to work with.

As you do this, make sure you are specific, that is, say exactly what your expectations are, and be very consistent.

Learn to give your child some space to breath . Do not suffocate him. Avoid doing what he can do for him. Do not enslave others to please your child, because those you enslaved, will one day be free and grow smarter than your child.

The moment you realize there is only one life to live, you will put everything you have into making sure that your child succeeds while you are still living.

(8) A MOTHER SHOULD ADMIT IT, WHEN SHE IS WRONG

Many mothers feel they are just too perfect to make any mistake but unfortunately, no one is perfect. Accepting it whenever you are wrong is an act of responsibility and accountability. It is even one of the principles of human relations. Remember that what you do not have, you cannot give; and what you do not know, you cannot teach. So the more responsible and accountable you are, the better for you to teach your child.

Do you know that it is pride that makes one not to admit a mistake. It is an act of pride that makes one feel too old to say sorry when there is need for it.

An humble person will be willing to say sorry to either a younger or older person that deserves it.

A Godly mother will follow the Godly principle of asking for forgiveness without being appealed to. The fact that you are the mother does not mean that you cannot go wrong or make any mistake.

Accepting it when you are wrong before your child earns you a huge respect and honor. It is an indication of showing dignity and respect for others and your child will learn this from you and show it to others.

THE MOTHER AND HER TEENAGE CHILD

Raising teenagers is not as bad and fearful as many mothers believe. Actually, if a mother based her mothering style on the pre-conceived ideas, such will pose a lot of danger for both the mother and the child. This is why, the bible emphasized that a child should be trained the way to go, so that, when he grows up, he will not depart from it.

A mother who wants to have peace at a later stage in life must learn to start training her child according to the words of God. A child who understands the word of God early in life, develops the fear of God in his heart which will guide him even in the midst of any temptation. Allow your child to learn to obey the words of God early in life. It is whatever is put into a child that he will grow up to live with.

Raising teenagers is not supposed to be done with force, fear or with pain. If you desire that your teenage child turns out good, your dependability must be on God for direction.

It is a training that should be handled with understanding, care, love, closeness, affection, empathy and above all, with the direction of God.

If your child is too scared of you, he/she will hide many things from you, hence mistakes will abound.

A mother cannot depend on her own understanding or power, to raise a successful teenager in today's society.

Your energy, strength, money, influence are not only what you need to raise a good teenager.

If you miss any of the aforementioned guidelines, it will be like throwing your teenage child into the pool without teaching him how to swim .This is the stage where your mothering style has to be less of authoritarian, but more of God's way. When you follow the

Godly way to handle your teenager, steps to take will be ordered by God, and you as the mother will not use the world's standard to rule him.

By using God's standard, your style of mothering him will be of less fatigue. You will be able to exercise your spiritual authority over him in a Godly way. Though, the authoritarian style has both its good and bad sides when handling a teenager, whichever way it goes, firmness and consistency helps ensure that every action you take, is objective and logical. A mother who feels she needs to be tougher with her teenage child, will be creating a non conducive atmosphere for both of them. Not being tough does not mean you are not in control over your child, it is in your interest to allow your teenager to breath some air of freedom, so that she can communicate with you in a more relaxed mood. If she is too scared of you, she will hide many things from you, hence mistakes abound.

Teenagers too go through a hard and difficult time with their peers. It is the age when they look for approval from friends and when acceptability means a lot to them. It is the age when they feel mothers are not fair to them, because of not approving all that they want to do. It is the age when they want to do what they feel like doing. It is the age that they feel their mothers are not understanding them. It is the age when some of them keep clothes or even some stuff outside the home because the mother is not ready to listen to them. If your relationship with your teenager is the cat and mouse kind, regret abounds. It is in your best interest to have good and honest conversation with your child all the time than for you to totally disapprove of her.

If all you do is to criticize your child, she will not bother to tell you anything. It is for you to let her know the reason why she cannot do what she requested from you. Create an avenue whereby both of you can reason together, and arrive at a logical conclusion.

Your teenager's interest is totally different from your own. You cannot exactly raise her the way you were raised. Yesterday's standard cannot be used for today's children. Life is changing.

As a matter of fact everything has changed. The way

> **If your relationship with your teenager is the cat and mouse kind, regret abounds.**

you communicate or show love to your teenage child is totally different from the way your own mother communicated with you. You will be missing it if you continue to use the old idea in totality to train these century children. Remember your motive is raisingyour teenager to be a responsible, God fearing adult.

This does not mean that old ways of raising children

should be totally condemned, but the fact is , children of old, were raised to obey the last order without any questioning. Children of today however want to understand the reason behind any action.

Most of the time, home is no longer a reflection of a child's behavior as many children live double standard kind of life. Many people wonder why a child from a good home so to say, goes out and turns to be wild. A good home in this contest may be likened to a Christian home, or a home where the parents are successful in their professions, or a home where the parents are affluent and they are not separated. All these are not all determining how a teenager will turn out to be. Gone are the days when it was the children of the single parent that were not doing well.

Various occurrences have proved this notion not to be true any longer. Instead, it is now turning the other way round where the children of married wealthy parents are getting into trouble more than before. This may be due to the fact that the children are being spoilt, or the parents are too pre-occupied with their professions, or the care of their children are left for their domestic workers.

Are you a mother who feels your teenager is too big to be corrected? If you are, then your child must have switched roles with you. It is the duty of a Godly mother to show her teenage child as to the way she dresses. A good start in the life of a child will end up well. How comfortable are you as a Godly mother looking at your teenage child dressing in a very promiscuous way?

There are better ways your teenage child can dress decently and neatly and still look good. Seductive dressing is not for children of God. If you have a difficult teenager who is proofing to know more than you do, learn to get on your knees as a mother for God's help. You should be able to identify your problem area before God can step into it for solution. There is nothing that is too small to pray to God about, most especially in the life of a child. It is your duty to seek the face of God so that your children's appearance will glorify God's name. If things go right from home, the world will be at peace.

Let us also face the fact about the teenage lifestyles that mothers need to understand, the fact is that every teenage child really wants to look good, even better than her older siblings. Your own definition of a good way of dressing or appearance may look boring or too dull for your teenage girl.

If you are the kind of a mother who will never listen to a child's suggestion, the child will withdraw and decide to do what she feels is right. You will never hear anything from her. Such a child may choose to keep her clothes in a friend's house and wear them outside of the home. Teenagers are very much concerned about their physical appearance and if you do not show concern and assist them to look right, you will lose them to some wayward friends who will help direct the affairs of your child. You will win the heart of your child, if you calm down to discuss issues with her.

If you give her your word of trust, she will be free to let you know what she wants to wear. After she might have told you, if you give reasons why such is not alright or appropriate, she will reason with you if you allow her to know what God expects of her, as His child. You need to let her be free to discuss her needs with you. Try not to always criticize her, let her realize that she has some positive contribution to make to the success of the home.

To avoid your teenage children from being depressed or having low self esteem, it is your duty to assist her. Teenage life is always full of conflicting issues. You need to understand that they face the peer group pressure among their friends at school, and even in the church.

Let me appeal to you mothers, the care of a child is not only in the area of feeding and education, it goes far beyond that. Your child's self esteem is also affected by her appearance. It is your responsibility as a mother to notice every physical change that takes place in her body, and be willing to take appropriate step to rise up to the responsibility of providing the necessary need. As soon as your teenage girl reaches puberty stage, there is possibility of her developing either acne or other skin related issues. Many mothers feel it is very irrelevant to assist their teenage girls take care of their skin most especially their faces.

Teenagers are very much into their physical appearance and if you do not show concern you will lose them to some wayward friends

Overlooking this aspect, will give your teenager low self esteem. Get her every necessary assistance before it gets out of control, the moment you help her look her best, she will appreciate your good role of motherhood. This action should not be seen as a bad exposure. You are doing your duty as a mother who cares

Avoiding it will dampen her morale and low self esteem is the result. Within a reasonable budget, you can choose to make your child look good.

Do not hide too many issues from your grown up child, because one day she will get to become a parent also. The moment she knows what you can afford, she will be reasonable with you. Mothers of today should learn to connect with their teenage children, because of the emotional issues they go through . The closer you are to your teenagers, the more they will be anxious to come home.

Learn to make your home a conducive place for your child to come to. Do not always shut down your teenagers. Let them talk with you, it is out of lengthy discussion that you will get to understand each other much better.

Even when she asks a question that looks scary to you, do not show any alarm. Calm down, hold your breath, and pray for wisdom before you respond, so that, she can feel comfortable to confide in you.
You can do a lot of reasoning to help your teenage child grow to be a responsible God fearing child if you so much desire. What you need is to mind the language and the choice of words to use because whatever you say is going to be taking seriously.

A Godly mother needs to give her teenage child sex education from home. Waiting to talk about sex education to your child should not wait till her teenage years. It should be done earlier in life. This is a way of providing your child with the necessary skills to better guide her decision making in life.

Such information and guidance will help them to appreciate the work of God and it will help them to know the importance of purity. You do not need to wait for the school or friends to train your child on this crucial topic. Instead of waiting for your child to be mis-guided, you are better off training her according to what the bible says concerning this topic. Many mothers, find it difficult to discuss the issue of sex with their children. As it is often said, *'experience is the best teacher"*. Forget about how terrible or good your own teenage life was, all you need to do now is to guide against allowing your child to sin or make mistakes.

If you do not want your child to be a victim of molestation, it is better for you to educate him or her. Tell him or her what the word of God says about holiness, and try as much as you can to protect them from any bad exposure.

Nowadays, some Godly mothers encourage their children to take birth control pill or use condom. Such mothers believe that it is impossible for girls in this generation to do without sex before marriage. Instead of preventing the sin, they take measures to avoid consequence.

What do we say to such mothers who call themselves Godly mothers? The ones who feel that certain things are impossible for God to do for their children. If you are such a mother, you need to go back to the basics of biblical doctrine and learn to accept all the biblical principles of raising a child for Christ. Though, there is temptation to compromise your Godly beliefs in other to satisfy the world, but as a mother, who are you expected to satisfy? Is it what the world is saying or what the word of God says about sex? Teach your child about abstinence, which means there should be

104

no sex before marriage. It is a great mistake for a Godly mother to encourage her child to use protective device for sexual activity. Let him/her realize how important his/he body is to God.

> **God's power is so precious to Him that He will not throw it away on just anybody. If you are not proven you won't know its value.**

The book of *1Thessalonians 4 : 3-4* says

> *" For this is the will of God, even your sanctification, that ye should abstain from fornication: That every one of you should know how to possess his vessel in sanctification and honor"*

The book of *1 Corinthians 6 :18-20* says,

> *" Flee from sexual looseness, any other sin which a man commits is one outside the body, but he who commits sexual immorality sins against his own body. Do you not know that your body is the temple of the Holy Spirit who lives within you, whom you have received from God? So then, honor God and bring glory to Him in your body."(Ampl.)*

In this regard, it is your duty to counsel your child according to the Biblical Principles because you will be accountable before God.

At the same time, your child is watching your back.

You need to realize that God gave you the child to guide in a proper way and not to pamper and destroy. You are to tell your child what he does not know and let him or her realize that it is only Godly Principle that can bring Godly result.

CHAPTER

MOTHERS' WILDERNESS EXPERIENCE: A NECESSARY CHALLENGE.

A wilderness is regarded as a place of desolation, loneliness, dis-satisfaction, mere existence, and where nothing seems to be happening at all.

Life is full of battles; anybody can start a thing, but it takes an achiever to complete it. It is necessary for every mother to know that between where she is and where God has promised to take her, there will be many stops, and at each stop is a different challenge. Each challenge has different part to play in your life.

For each challenge you encounter along the way, there is a lesson which God wants you to learn. What determines whether you will be successful during the battle is who you depend upon as your helper. For you to end well in life, the beginning will be rough.

Have you seen anyone who is very wealthy or attain a prominent position without having a story to tell? None that I know of. There is bound to be challenges in life. For gold to come out shinning, it must pass through fire. There is no need to die before seeing the real death. God has a purpose for making you a woman.

Every woman has a wilderness experience which she either had passed through or is still passing through, or will pass through in the future. Given the inevitability of passing through a wilderness at one time or the other , the good news that I have for you is that, all the experiences learned will simply prepare you for the prominent places that God has prepared for you.

Poverty is war, bondage is war, barrenness is war, separation is war, divorce is war, widowhood is war, sickness is war because they all shut you up in a cage. They all rob you of the right to freedom of speech. Who on earth is ready to listen to a poor man's idea? What idea does he want to give that will be beneficial to anybody? No one is exempted from trouble; one may have her own time of persecution or rejection early in life, while others may have theirs later.

Going through all the rough roads makes your preparation for future attainment to be complete. The greater the chal- lenges you face, the greater your success; if your dependency

Every woman has a wilderness experience which she either had passed through or is still passing through, or will pass through in the future.

is only on God. For you not to fail, you need to get yourself together, and pray to God to give you strength for the journey ahead of you.

The book of *Isaiah 43:19* says:
"Behold , I will do a new thing, now it shall spring forth; shall ye not know it? I will Even make a way in the wilderness, and rivers in the desert".

This is the assurance we have if we believe in Him. As His chosen women, we must have the realization that He will never allow us to go through a wilderness without providing an escape route for us if we have strong faith in Him.

For any woman to become great, she must be ready to fight and win a great battle because the devil has not changed the method of deceit which he used on Eve. Therefore, mothers, do not underestimate the devil, because his interest is to destroy your testimony. As a woman, in which of these wilderness are you? Is it the wilderness of sickness, broken marriage, barrenness, loneliness, separation, being jilted, suffering in silence, joblessness, raising children alone, or widowhood?

Is your situation making you to weep secretly? Are you being looked down upon, or wrongly judged as a result of the situation you find yourself? Are the blessings of God in your life becoming a big issue for your enemies to fathom? Probably, your own issue is as a result of a particular sex of children. Can you imagine that many are never satisfied?

I wonder why such should be an issue for anybody, after all, God is the only creator of life. He already knows the end from the beginning, and He has never made a mistake. He chooses to bless you the way He likes. May be the enemies are even angry for your silence, because silence is the best for them when you know that God is on the throne watching everyone; moreover, He says He is the only unseen fighter - without any weapon.

Jesus had people around Him in the garden of Gethsemane, but He was still lonely and in serious agony. May be you are living in a very big and bea

110

tiful house, yet you are sorrowful and lonely. Many drive big cars, wear good outfits and still they are miserable and empty inside. All the pains and fears that came as a result of the challenges you face could only be touched by God. Despite everybody being with Him at Gethsemane, He was sorrowful. To reach your destiny in life, to be able to raise a fulfilled child, there will always be pain and fear along the way.

The moment you believe that the pains, fear, and fleshy problems you go through that Jesus passed through them and passed everything, you too will get to achieve your goals , your children shall come out well to reach their set destiny.

Walking and trusting with God is a hard thing as it demands keeping pace with Him always. You can't go too fast or go too slow.

If you have been saying, this is too much, I can't bear it anymore, you are not embracing your Godly choice, if you do not relent and bear the pain, you will not reach the set goal. No matter how sorrowful it is, pray to God to give you the strength to go through the season and survive it.

There might be falling of leaves now, but you should know that the moment it is spring, the whole leaves will spring up. Just continue to pray to God to let His will be done because if it is God's will for you to get your destiny, not your desire, you will certainly be celebrated. Jesus' desire was not to go to the cross, He prayed against it, but the will of God had to be done.

There is always a season of *"things not happening"* during ones wilderness season, but believe that there is a land of milk and honey awaiting for you ahead. During the hurdles of life, if you allow your flesh to rule you, you will never attain your Godly destiny. Looking at the story of the blind Baltimaeus in the books of **Luke 18:35-43**; and **Mark 10;46-52**; many of us go through rough roads because we do not know the God we serve as the God that darkness cannot withstand. His reaction to darkness is to bring light at any point in time. The blind man has been sitting for years at the same spot begging but when the day his season of deliverance came , he shouted for mercy with all his strength and energy, and Jesus heard him. Though people tried to shut him down, he persisted and shouted until something happened.

The book of **Mathew 11:12** says :
> *"And from the days of John the Baptist until now,*
> *The kingdom of God suffereth violence,*
> *and the violent that take it by force"*.

Unless force is used, the devil will never allow any-body to have anything good. Force is making some-thing that is not happening to happen by all means.

Going through a terrible experience in the wilderness will certainly make you to desire an urgent change. To reverse a curse, you need force. To alter a direction, there must be a re- route somewhere.

To change your life situation for the better, you need to force the change to happen. Queen Esther forced a change to happen; She confidently said *'If I perish, I perish*, without any fear of the consequence. Delilah used her own persuasion in a negative way to destroy Samson, Ahab was steered up to wickedness by his wicked wife.

> **To alter a life's direction, there must be a re-routed plan visible to everyone somewhere, that will change the situations in your life.**

A lazy person will desire for a long time and will never find the way out. That is why you find many people who die wishing. Change takes more than just wishing. When there is a desire to do something, it should be followed up with an action. If your situation does not please you, you have to forcefully change it by yourself in place of prayer. Therefore, the wilderness period is the time for you to recreate your life to what you want it to look like. If you fold your hands and keep complaining, the devil will defeat you. You must forcefully say "No", to the devil by letting him know that your change is not negotiable. There is no winner without a battle.

The book of *Job 14:1* says,
> *"Man that is born of a woman is of few days, and full of trouble".*

The most important thing is to prepare to war with the kingdom of hell. There is no change without a price. Jesus Christ offered His life as a change for us all. For you to get out of the wilderness, your own price may be sleepless nights of prayer, to others, it may include fasting; to some people, it may be pride. Namaan dropped his pride before healing came his way.

Nothing good can come easy. What could Hannah have done, without a Peninnah? Thank God because Hannah became angry and she forced her change to come in the place of prayer. I think everybody should thank God for every Peninnah in their lives. At least someone has to provoke you for you to know that you cannot continue to be on the same spot anymore. You need to step out of the neighborhood of desire, I wish I could. Enough is enough .

As a mother, if your child is wayward, does not know how to stay at home, talks back to you rudely, follows bad gangs, does not have any respect for anyone; you

114

need to enforce a change in the place of fasting and praying. You need to rededicate the child unto God who is able to turn every bad situation around.

The book of *11Chronicles 20:15b* says:
"Be not afraid nor dismayed by reason of this great multitude, For the battle is not yours."

With these words, any mother that is going through her own period of wilderness, needs not be afraid. You must be of good courage, because your maker does not sleep nor slumber.

All you need to believe is that, no matter how long you work, there will be a night of rest. No matter what the enemy brings your way, it is only God who has the last say over your life, so, it can never be over until God says it is over. No matter how big or stinking your own dry bone is, God has a way of putting flesh into it.

The same way God heard the groaning of the children of Israel, and remembered His covenant with Abraham, Isaac, and with Jacob, He will listen to all your groaning and secret tears. He will remember His covenants of peace, blessing, healing, companionship, and fruitfulness, over you and release you from any form of bondage the devil has put you. When the Israelites were in the slavery for over 400 years, it was like they had been forgotten, but when the time of their favor came, God sent Moses on an errand of deliverance and they were set free. He does not forget His own, therefore wait for your own time. When you are going through the challenges of life, you need to get yourself ready for where God is taking you to. Be expectant of the changes that will come your way. You must guide against anything that will cause you not to receive the blessings prepared for you.

As a child of God, your wilderness period is a ladder you need to climb to your greatness. God wants you to realize that if people help you out of your problem, they will take the glory, and even share it with others but when God helps you, He never discuss you with anyone. He will take you out of the mess because of His love for you.

All you need is to hand over your problem to Him with absolute trust and go to sleep. He is willing to watch over you like a mother watches over her little baby. Looking unto men will prolong your stay in the wilderness. For God to uplift you, He has to test your heart to know if your total dependency is in Him or not.

To be an Ultimate mom, you must be willing to go through extra-ordinary problems.

You must be willing to fight extra- ordinary battles. Sometimes, God needs to allow you to go through a wilderness to get your attention towards Him or to save you from destruction.

116

Looking back to my life experience, I have every cause to thank Jehovah God for the Peninnahs of my life. I have had so many of them, but I thank God for using them to push me to my destiny. They provoked me to look for Jesus, and depend on Him for everything.

They made me to be hungry for the Savior, In fact they pushed me to a stage where my total dependency was only on God alone. Without my wilderness experience, I would have been totally lost, but God found me and made me to know that He is more than able, and that He is the only one who can do all things.

I think I need to share a little bit of my wilderness experience. The enemies thought they had done their best, not knowing that where they stopped was where my miracles were starting from. I laid my petitions before my maker, by reporting every incident in tears and with a broken heart. God was just too merciful and he still is. He took me out of their fiery furnace, out of the dungeon of life where the enemies tried to keep me.

He lifted me up and blew His freshness into my nostrils. He rebuilt me and gave me double for my trouble.

He proved to my goliath that he was small. He restored every thing that the locust and cankerworm stole from me in an imaginable way. God is just too good. He proved Himself as God who rules in the affairs of men. He proves Himself as God who is bigger than what people think or say.

God put laughter in my mouth, He made me have joy like a river, He made me to be a pillar and not a Caterpillar. As I praise Him on a daily basis, there is always a miraculous release of His power. And all the other miracles that are hidden or buried begin to show up for me. His favor becomes geometrical for me and I no longer operate with a grasshopper mentality. The experience I had, taught me to pray without ceasing.

Do you blame God when everything is not working? Perhaps, there is something He wants you to learn from the mess.

It made me enjoy praying like eating. It made me believe that no one can understand the details of how God works. This is part of what makes Him to be God.

Do you feel like Joseph who was sold out as a result of family problem? Or you feel like you are in the pit today, empty or lonely. Does everything around you seem dry? You are not by yourself. It takes the promise of God to make a woman to keep going on in the time of adversity. God wants you to praise Him, even when your expectations are not yet met. Do you

118

blame God when your marriage is not working? Perhaps, there is something He wants you to learn from the mess. Joseph did not blame anybody for his problem, instead, he rose above the issues. He put away self pity. Joseph knew it was God who placed him in Portiphar's house, hence, he said, he would not do a bad thing against God. Why don't you think of what God has done for you and continue to appreciate Him for all. Do not worry about those things He has not done. Imagine the way Joseph was imprisoned because of righteousness.

His imprisonment was in the plan of God, because, if he did not go ,there was no way he would have gotten to know King Pharaoh. He did not know that his jail term was a way to greater joy. Following God can sometimes be confusing but except you really have to trust in Him. He is God and He will continue to be God, no matter what. In an attempt to raise your child in a Godly way, nothing must be too precious for you to give up.

In the midst of whatever you go through, try to see God in it. The devil may attack you, and your children but do not allow any irrelevant thing to distract you. Set your eyes upon your ultimate goal and vision for survival. You should not allow the devil to make you believe that you cannot get out of any ugly situation. You must believe that you will still be celebrated. Because problems become more intense does not make God to stop being God. Sometimes, when you are cheated, and you do not react, the devil thinks you are weak, not knowing that it takes a lot of understanding and strength for you not to fight back. The devil knows what to attack, that will not allow you to move out of bondage, hence, you need to be wise. Can you just imagine the kind of ugly presentation the devil gave Eve in the garden of Eden. He must have tried to convince Eve by saying that God tried to hide certain things from them. Probably, he has been telling you that kind of a lie to let you have mistrust in God. May be he has been telling you, *"Are you still there praying?"*

Is God worth waiting upon after these years of your barrenness? You know what? For you to know what somebody is capable of doing, you would wish to check his past record or resume. What is it that the devil has done in the past that is not counterfeit? What has he done that is not full of deceit? What has he given that he does not collect back in double?

There is no measurable stage to compare our God with the devil in terms of any thing. God is not man, the way He told Jehosaphat, that he would fight for him, and he would have his peace, He did it. The devil will leave you to go through your trouble alone, he will hide when you are going through it, and he will wait for you to self destroy your destiny once you trust in him more than God.

If God was able to deliver the Israelites from Egypt after 430 years of slavery, how big is your own problem that you feel He can not solve? The Israelites got to Marah where the water was bitter and God told Moses to point his rod to the river to become sweet for them to drink. This is another assurance that your bitter life will one day become sweet for the world to see.

You may feel discouraged, neglected or even abandoned, it may even look like it is not going to be alright anymore, but, let me tell you, God is working on it. He treasures you so much that He cannot make you to be an abandoned property. Sometimes, God needs to take certain things that make us to be arrogant in order to humble us.

The book of ***Romans 8 :35*** says that
  "nothing can separate us from the love of Christ."

If Christ be for you in the midst of problems, even when your child is proving difficult for you to handle, nothing should separate you from Him, because He loves and cherishes you.

Romans 8:28 says,
  ***"all things work together for good to them
          that love God."***
Learn to cast all your burden unto Him for He cares. The devil has nothing good to offer any body.

121

Whatever he rushes into your hand has an expiry date. God's miracle is for ever.

WHAT MAKES THE WILDERNESS EXPERIENCE LONGER?

The book of *Hosea 4:6* says:
"My people perish for lack of knowledge".

In all that you do in life, knowledge and the use of wisdom are the key things. The more knowledge you get, the more the authority you can use. Knowledge is the only thing that can chase ignorance away. Actually, another word for ignorance can also be darkness. Knowledge is the key that can unlock closed doors to take you to a higher level. It is with knowledge that you can dig deep into the source of your problem.

A soldier can not go to a battle without a prior knowledge of the enemies' information. It is the information that will guide his preparation for the war ahead of him.

Knowledge is the key that can unlock closed doors to take you to a higher level. Seek knowledge and grow strength

---

The information you get will enable you to better face any issue that is ahead of you. Lack of knowledge will cause you to perish easily in the wilderness.

122

Believing in the resurrection power of God, and acquiring the necessary tools in the place of prayer the journey in the wilderness will become smoother for you to exit safely. If God can assist David to bring Goliath down, who is that person standing like a mountain in front of you that God cannot bring down? Who can battle with the Lord? I can confidently say *'NOBODY'*.

For your journey not to be prolonged in the wilderness, you need to have the right weapons to use. Necessary information will accelerate your way out of the wilderness and your prolonged years will become years of new opportunity. You will then become a faster runner because you will outrun those who went ahead of you.

The favor of God will cause you to reach where He ordained for you. When the power of God touches you, the size of your Goliath will not matter at all. His power will make you to do the extraordinary things. You need to seek knowledge in order not to fight amiss. Sometimes the root cause of your problem is in your foundation. Some people's lives have been mortgaged by their parents unconsciously but no matter how bad the foundation is, it is never too big for God to change completely
Going to the root of ones foundation can help one get solution to every long standing issues so that such do not occur in the lives of the children. You need

a clean heart and genuine repentance to break the yoke that evil foundations brought into your life. The moment you confess your sins, it is absolutely necessary never to go back into such sins anymore.

Many times, you find yourself roaming around for too long in the wilderness of life because you do not have the knowledge of what brought you there in the first place. Who knows, probably, you have been wandering for so long in that wilderness as a result of some issues surrounding your birth.

Do you know how desperate your parents looked for you? Do you know who was consulted for you to be born? Do you know the vows they made for you to be alive? Do you know where they got your name from? Do you know the star readers they consulted to search for your future? Do you know whether you are named after a very terrible and wicked, person?

The moment you reflect back on these mentioned factors, to deal with your prolonged journey in the wilderness of life will become easy, because you will know how to deliver yourself out of the dungeon. Jacob wrestled and got his deliverance and his name was changed to Israel. The genesis of your child's bad behavior may be as a result of your own birth issue. The devil does not have the right to hold you down when God is ready to deliver you. As soon as you are delivered, God will give you a new name and life will be easy for both you and your child. You will enjoy

124

raising him according to the plan of God. Every tree that God has not planted in you shall surely be uprooted. Amen!

Is your wilderness experience a marital issue or having a wayward child ?You may need to re-visit your foundation to be able to pray aright. What is the foundation of your marriage based upon?

How about your mother's marriage? Is your mother the 'other woman' who used every means to enter into her marriage?

Did you do the same thing? Are you aware of the fact that

The genesis of your child's bad behavior may be as a result of your own birth issues.

God says, what ever He has joined together nothing or nobody must put asunder?

Every woman needs to go back to re-visit the journey of her life. If you caused others to weep for you to enjoy, God is not a man so He cannot be fooled. If you pull a person down to attain her rightful position, you need to repent, restore and restitute. This may be too tough to do, but the word of God is true, nothing can be added or deducted from it.

Living right is what brings profitable result. Though, you may have thousands of reasons to justify your actions, but are the actions in line with what the word of God says about marriage? No one is given the mandate to judge any other fellow, but, consider the feelings of God concerning every step you have taken in life. . He is a merciful God, who is more than willing to forgive and cleanse everyone that comes to Him with a genuine heart; however, you cannot continue your life in a sinful act and wants grace to continue to abound.

It is not difficult for God to bring your wayward child back home, nor hard for Him to speak to the wind troubling your life to be still. It took Abraham twenty five years to wait and God fulfilled His promises concerning him and Sarah. Though, He is very merciful, but you have to repent genuinely and do things according to God's principles. Putting others in agony for you to be happy is not biblical for a child of God.

The book of *1 Corinthians 3:11* says,
"For other foundation can no man lay than that is laid, which is Jesus Christ".

Any foundation that is laid on sin, can never be solid, though.
If Jesus went to hell for three days to fight, disgrace, and to seize all the powers from the devil to come and lay new foundation for us, It does not matter the depth of the foundation that your problem is rooted into, the word of God is the divine harmer, powerful and sharper than anything. If the nostril of God can divide the red sea, you should know that He is ready to set

you free from the cage you have been locked in for so long. All you need to do is to make your stand clear in Christ so that He will set into your battle to fight for you.

The most important thing is for your story to change. You cannot enter into the presence of God with a filthy hand, so you need His mercy to wash you clean from either your own sin or that of your parents. You need God to give you a total new life. It is always God's nature to be merciful to His people. If you sow mercy, you will definitely reap mercy.

Sometimes, you are at the brink of your fulfillment, when the spirit known as the spirit of non completion shows up, to make you return back to the original point in the wilderness where you started from. This is the spirit that makes one to start and not to finish right.

It brings sorrow to ones life. This kind of spirit can originate as a result a rugged foundation. This is a spirit that will make somebody to have children, train the children, set the children up for every good thing if life, but when it is time for the mother to settle down and begin to enjoy the fruit of her labor, something tragic will either happen to the child or the mother. It is a spirit that every mother needs to rebuke all the time. It is the spirit that causes divorce, separtion, terminal disease, loneliness, in ones life.

The book of **Deuteronomy 3:27**, God said to Moses:

"Get thee up into the top of Pisgah, and lift up
thine eyes westward, and northward,
and southward, and eastward,
and behold it with thine eyes:
for thou shall not go over this Jordan"

To Moses, that was a mountain where he was shown the promised land ahead of him, but that, he would not get there. God made it clear to Moses, upon Mt. Pisgah where he could see everything, but, he would not proceed.

By every reason, Moses was a good example by God, but he was overtaken by the disobedience and complainsof Israelites. The spirit that cuts one off at the peak of ones enjoyment is the spirit that operates at that mountain.

To any woman in the wilderness, that spirit can make you stay there for a long time, or even make you get tired and perish in the wilderness. The moment you come to this reality of this kind of a spirit, it is for you who wants to end the race of mothering, and finish it well, to borrow a leaf from this. While in the wilderness, you need to know what will not make you finish well, and guide against it.

For Moses, he was overtaken by anger through the disobedience and complains of the Israelites. God stopped him from entering into the promised land upon all the toiling he did from Egypt through the wilderness.

As a mother, do not allow anger or provocation disallow you from getting out of the wilderness.

Enemies attack those who are very close to their destiny. Under the darkness of your life is the raw material that you need to bring you out to the pre- destined place. It is the duty of every woman to persistently pray against the spirit of non-completion. God will grant us all the spirit to begin and finish well in Jesus name.

Backsliding is like going back to ones vomit. The devil is always looking for who to win over to his demonic kingdom, you should not allow your challenges make you seek another god. Your waiting time may seem too long to you, one thing you need to realize is that, there is time for everything. At God's own time, not your own time, your story will change. That child will come back home just like the prodigal child did.

The balm of Gilead shall touch every pain and you shall be totally free from every oppression. God who opened the wombs of Sarah, Hannah, and Elizabeth is still on the throne. He will surely replace whatever needs any replacement in your body. Learn to endure, be consistent, and fervent in your prayer. Jesus prayed before taking any step , so, we need to put prayer first before embarking on any endeavor. It is not how well or how early you start a journey that matters, it is how well it is ended, therefore it is he who laughs last, that will surely laugh best.

To get out of the various challenges as a woman, the only way that is sure and permanent is through Jesus Christ. There is no Christianity without the cross. To defeat the devil, you must be ready to carry your cross.

The road to follow is always a narrow and lonely road. It takes a lot of courage, tolerance and persistence to pass through successfully. Each woman's dry bone differs in size, stinks differently, but when God is ready to let all the bones receive flesh, He does it permanently without thinking about the size or how long it has been there. You have to determine to work hard to come out of any type of wilderness issues you find yourself so that the gift of God does not become a reproach for you.

On that day before God, what will you have to tell Him about the children He gave to you as free gifts? Abraham passed the test of time before God, that is why God called him His friend.

You must plan to step into a new way of life and determine to drop every excess baggage of sin so that you can become light to move fast with Jesus. Let your life pattern change to the original pattern that God original designed for you and your life will never remain the same again in Jesus name.

SINGLE MOTHERS SHALL BOUNCE BACK AGAIN

Single motherhood can be caused either by the death of a husband, separation, divorce or having a child without being married.

Despite the scriptural facts concerning marriage as laid down in the bible, divorce or separation came into existence as a result of the hardness of hearts of the parties concerned which was not in the original plan of God. Some cultures belief that marriage is a necessary evil; even when one or both parties are not

willing to be committed. When every attempt for rec-
onciliation fails, it is considered appropriate the victim of this circumstance not to give up, but continue
to be fervent in the place of prayer for restoration.
Therefore, in whichever way she is called to serve in
the house of God, let that be her priority.

Any woman who is in this category should not be put
under more rejection through condemnation. I bet, no
one wants to hear this, but it is sometimes necessary
to emphasize it because in some cultures or societies,
a single mother is looked down to as a social leper or
an outcast.

The moment one is able to address the cause of the
situation biblically, the rest should be left in the hands
of God.

Finding yourself in this category should not make you
lose your head, your worth, or your integrity as a
mother and above all as a child of God. Like I said
earlier, after you consciously did what you were supposed to do as a child of God , then stand right. Do not
lose your soul for the devil. Sometimes, you cannot
do anything about what you have lost, but you can do
a lot to hold on and plan to have a better future. Align
yourself with the Lord.

You should keep your good reputation and guard your
self worth. Setting your self aside for the work of God
should be your greatest priority. It is the time for you
to pray for the grace of God to abound to make the

experience worthy of joyful praise at the end of it all by getting your self back to the track The moment you refuse to allow the tribulation or distress to separate you from the love of Christ, then the devil has lost a candidate.

The book of *James 1:2* says,
"Consider it pure joy, my brothers, whenever you face trials of many kinds because you know that the testing of your faith develops perseverance"

The right responses in the midst of trouble always minimize regrets. One of the ways of bouncing back successfully, is to go through the troubled time in such a way that you can look back and realize that there was no shame in the way you managed to get out of the trouble. The way you handled your wilderness moment will determine how remarkable you are as a mother.

You must know that the wilderness period for a child of God who has a destiny to fulfill is always guarded by God's permission. He always turns such experience to a period of growth for His glory to manifest at the end of it. God's truth will never change, regardless of how we feel. No matter how ugly or messy the situation is, you must have the assurance that God has a better future for you. This is a period of re- routing your plan towards the right direction. It is the period

THE ULTIMATE MOM; Your God Given Assignment

of seeking the face of God like never before for His original plan for your life. It is not a period for calling a pity party, condemning yourself or playing a blaming game because listening to people's comment, ideas and suggestions will discourage you. It is only God , who can give you the best direction of how to rise up, after you have fallen down.

The easiest way to bounce back is for you to go back to the basic foundation of the plans of God for your life. How and Where? This could only be found through the word of God. As you search the scriptures, with regards to God's promises concerning you, your present circumstances, your children's lives, and how you can best handle them, your life and that of your children will be back to normal.

The good news I have for you is that, God knows about the journey of your life, therefore, there is no condemnation of any kind for you the moment you are in Christ Jesus. The moment you accept Him as your savior, take directives from Him, He will continue to rule every affair of your life according to His will. He will make every crooked way straight. Even if you attained the single motherhood, through personal mistakes, with genuine repentance, He will restore everything that you lost. You should be fully persuaded that what He has promised, He will surely perform. Put your trust in Him who is the author and finisher of your faith.

He is the ever present help in times of need. Though being single may make you have a set back, fear, mistrust, self doubt, self blame and regret, God is in all of it.

Due to the situation, sometimes you may be laughing on the outside while crying on the inside. Or, may be the man you thought you knew very well stabbed you in the back. Or he just became a total stranger for no just cause. Or, you were forced out because of another woman. Probably, you unknowingly made a wrong decision by getting involved in a wrong relationship.

You know what, until you are able to drop the excess baggage of negative thought, it will be difficult for you to get your life back on track.

> **Drop the excess baggage of negative thought, or it will be difficult for you to get your life back on track**

Your help is in the hands of the Almighty who is your maker. You should be grateful to God for keeping you alive. Do you know that being alive to testify to God's goodness poses a terror to the kingdom of darkness ? The devil whose duty is to destroy, does not know how to restore or repair. God had already promised that He will restore all that the enemies had taken from you. When He restores, it is going to be more than what you lost. He is going to give you double for your trouble. Reasoning it out for God is like seizing

135

His power from Him. As the all knowing God, if He was able to raise the dead, what is it that He can not do for you?

Whatever lessons God wants you to learn from the episode is ideal for you so that you do not fall into such ugly situation again.

You should consider the situation as a joyful one, because God is in it with you. The joy of knowing Him, even in the midst of chaos is more than enough for you. Of what value will every thing be for you to have it all and lose your salvation. Continue to hold on to Him, seek Him diligently, and every other thing will be given to you. This means that you should realize that your troubled time is over , because God is the Ever present help in times of trouble.

It is not the time to ask "Why, What or Who caused it? It is the time to develop and grow in faith. To avoid double tragedy, it is the time for you to face your children and make sure you succeed in raising them. That is when your overnight weeping can bring joy in the morning. The moment you realize that victory is the best revenge for your adversaries, then you will work towards living a life that is worthy of God's glory. To have victory over every principality and power, and the rulers of darkness is what you need.

In the process of putting your life back on the track, you have to allow God to fight your battle for you, He will do it beyond your expectation. You must learn to forgive, so that you can be totally free. Doing all these will give you the peace to face your children and raise them in the way of God. You must not fail in the nurturing of your child. With God on your side, its going to be easy for you to do.

Try not to sin against God by committing adultery.

The bible says in the book of Romans 8:6, that :
" For to be carnally minded is death; but to be spiritually minded is life and peace."

It further said in verse 8 of the same passage that
"They that are in flesh cannot please God."

When you are in the spirit, you will do what is pleasing to God.
The sin against your body does not bring solution to your loneliness. It will kill your dream. Remember your body is the temple of God. The moment you have accepted Jesus Christ as your Lord and Savior, it means you are allowing God to be the architect of your life. You are no longer the owner of your life. Wherever God directs your life, that is where you should go.

Whatever He condemns as sin, must be condemned by you. Once you have decided to follow Him, you cannot act the way you feel, but the way the owner of

137

your life feels. It is His report you have to accept as the final. Choosing to enjoy the pleasure of the moment has its own effect. Whenever an evil deed is covered with pretense, heaven will record it. You must let your old behavior be crucified with Our Lord Jesus Christ, allow your body of sin be destroyed, so that sin will be stinking to you.

Here, we need to quickly have an overview of the other existing category of single mothers for clarity. Here, I am going to cut it deeper again. Were you the other woman? Did you play the game of robbing Peter to pay Paul? Did you push the children who should be in the palace into the street, for you to enjoy other people's sweat? Heaven will set such children free.

> **Whenever an evil deed is covered with pretense, Heaven will record it.**
> *Don't be fooled!!!*

Did you almost behave like Jezebel to get to the position you are right now?

The blood of Jesus shed on the Calvary is still fresh to deliver you if you repent of your sin. Or, you even got to the stage of operating in the Delilah spirit. Is the weeping of others giving you joy and satisfaction? Would you wish either you or your child be paid back in the same coin? Fellow mothers, let the answers to these questions be silently answered between you and God.

No matter what, He is still a God of second chance. The truth of the matter is, if your silent answers demand that you repent and make amends , even if it is for the sake of the children you have in that relationship, you need to do so. Above all, you may need to repent also because God does not want the death of a sinner, but for her to repent, and turn away from her iniquity.

Your salvation matters to God, because, heaven is real, and hell is also real. You cannot continue to sin , that grace should abound. It is not worth satisfying your flesh here on earth, and such flesh and soul to end in hell fire. Many people wrongfully justifies their bad behavior, it is simple common sense that you cannot out smart God.

It is never too late to retrace your steps because there is no sin He cannot forgive. If you need to restitute, do it for the sake of making heaven. Postponing this may be too late. He is the owner of your life, and He can do anything He wants with it. If you eventually choose not to repent, then, your pay day shall surely come when you will get the wages for your deed. I think a word is quite enough for the wise. If you have missed it as a mother, through any ungodly behavior, the blood of Jesus is still available to wash every sin away and make you clean again. It would not be appropriate to transfer any problem upon your child. You do not need to register your child in the school of failure.

You must always remember that somebody is watching your back. You know that heaven sees what a prophet cannot see. Allow God to rule the affairs of your life, and you will never miss it. To obey God is not always easy, cause He will instruct you to do some silly things which do not make sense to you. No matter the unpleasant situation you found yourself, it is for awhile if you can wait patiently in the place of persistent prayer and obedience. Jesus prayed against going to the cross, but God still made Him go.

There is always a season of *"things not happening"* in ones life. May be you looked for someone to share your burden or pain with, and no one showed up, Jesus was left alone on the way to the cross. In whichever way the ball of single motherhood rolls into your cot, the bottom line is that God is in the situation with you.

Though, the situation may look messy, shameful and lonely, God still knows about it all. Whatever, scenarioyour own situation falls into, God wants you to put all the excess load you are carrying aside because it is not your own. He wants you to cast your burden unto Him, for He cares. The moment He has forgiving you, you should completely run away from sin,

140

because you cannot continue to enjoy sin for grace to abound.

It may look hard to go on when every thing you depended upon fell apart around you. Regardless of how it happened or who was responsible for it, it is for you to pick your pieces together and allow God's grace to be sufficient for you. Though, it is much harder to raise a child single handedly, but, the fact still remains that, you must not lose the man, and also fail in the area of raising your child very well. It will become a double tragedy if you failed in this area. As you choose to train your child with loving and tender-discipline, the child's determination to succeed in life will make him develop to be a responsible adult even in the absence of a man.

You need to go back to the basic foundation of how to raise your child in a Godly way.
Being a single mother should not be an excuse for you, because the bible makes it clear that you can do all things, through Christ who strengthens you. The moment you determine to do it, God will back you up. Complaining or talking will not help you. Instead, it will compile your problem, and it will be hard for you to pray. Get yourself ready for the job ahead of you, and plan to be successful in it. If your child turns out to be good, you will forget your past hurt and pain.

It is time for you to fix your life. It is time for you to use your common sense before doing anything. You should not behave like the trouble is going to kill you. You should believe in the word of God. Create time to study the word of God for direction.

Do not only seek counsel from people who are in the same situation with you.

Try to confess His word, think right, and believe right. Always encourage yourself in the Lord that you are coming out of the trouble one day. Learn to confess the positive through your belief that as you get up from your fall, you will come up better.

Wisdom is always better than warfare, so, if you need help, seek it wisely.

Do not only seek counsel from people who are in the same situation with you. Do not follow the association of people who are negative thinkers. The kind of company you keep in the time of trouble determines how long you stay in the problem.

You should detach yourself from every evil association. To receive the wind of God, you have to move with Godly people. Learn to move with visionary people, because, they will be busy exploring better opportunities.

Abraham's promises never came to manifestation, until he separated with Lot. Learn to associate with people who have dreams. Always believe that with God all things are possible.

Learn to get rid of the fear that you know cannot make things possible. The more you keep trying, the more you become better. Until a child overcomes fear, he will not be able to walk. After he falls many times, he will one day pick up the courage to push himself for-ward to walk. You must learn to overcome the time of falling to succeed in any endeavor.

Depression is an enemy to your faith. Learn to be a positive thinker. The way you think will produce the way you feel, and the way you feel will definitely dictate the way you act. Whatever you keep too long in your mind will weigh you down, hence communicate with wise people.

Depression is evidence to lack of faith and an enemy to your faith

The book of *John 14:1* says
" Let not your heart be troubled; ye believe in God, believe also in me"

This indicates that you have control as to what you want to do with your heart. You can control your heart

143

from being troubled. You can as well be in the midst of trouble and not be troubled. You must accept the responsibility by controlling your heart. The moment you realize that wrong thinking will produce wrong belief, and your wrong belief will produce a wrong behavior, then you will choose to stabilize your self.

Learn to speak to your problem rather than speak about your problem. Instead of talking about the ugly situation, it is better to look at it in the face, and command it to move in the name of Jesus.

Mark 11:23, says
"That whatsoever shall say unto this mountain, be thou removed, and be thou cast into the sea, and shall not doubt in his heart, but shall believe that those things which he shall come to pass, he shall have whatsoever he saith".

With this, you should know that there is power in words. As you continue to raise your child, plan to go back to basic foundation of God's plan for you. You must know that He did not create you to suffer. His plans are for good and not of evil t take you and your child to an expected end. God's expected end for you is to have rest, peace, joy and all provisions.

Where you think is ended, is where God is starting with you. The basic fundamental of your creation is all you need to hold on to, which is, creating you to

144

have sufficiency, and for Him to satisfy you in all ways. Key into all His promises for you and teach your child the same thing. Feed him on the word of God.

Let him know that there is a conse-quence for any behavior. Spend your quality time with him, and he will appreciate you.

Teach your child to have all his depend-ency on God for sufficiency. Let Him know that God is the only constant friend who does not desert nor disap-point someone. The moment a child is rooted in the word of God, training him will be easy. Both of you will be able to speak the same language. You must learn to win in this time of trouble.

Whatever you keep too long in your mind will weigh you down, hence communicate with wise people.

Learn to move with visionary people, because, they will constantly be exploring better opportunities and new ideas that will improve your life.

Communicate with people that have wisdom. Divide your time between you and your child. Avoid being selfish to yourself or to your child.

Make good use of the time at hand. If you need to get more education or training, do not relent. Let your child be very proud of you as a mother.

Living in the past is the enemy of the future, so learn to move on with your life.

At the end of the day , your child will call you blessed and before you know it, you have already bounced back to your feet in a Godly manner.

MOTHERS NEVER GIVE UP

Choosing not to give up in the midst of every ugly circumstance is the best decision a mother can make to succeed in the race. Such a decision brings reformation which is an indication of going far and beyond the limitation of the devil.

Waiting is not always a palatable thing to do, but it pays on the long run. Though you might be experiencing many discouraging situations during the time, but it is still good to wait. If you give up, it means you have accepted a defeat. Quitting means you are tired of waiting on God for a solution, which means, you are considering other sources for solution. Waiting for His time means you want your result to be Him and not any other person. Actually, it is because of someone like you that Jesus left His kingdom to come and mend your broken heart, and to give you liberty from your oppressor.

As you decide to wait for God to show forth in your situation, you are definitely calling Him your healer, your provider, miracle worker, and a favored God. Choosing Him only, will involve a lot of stretching with pain, but it is going to produce joy that will last for ever, and even for your unborn generations to enjoy.

Choosing to hold on means choosing to keep trusting God on daily basis, even when it seems like there is no solution coming your way. As a mother who chooses to be successful at all cost, one needs to align her self with God , because choosing to do this is not only going to affect you alone, but your generations unborn.

Whatever makes you weep in your closet shall soon be over as you continue to wait patiently. God has to re-position you for you to get to your final destination, He has to re-plant you and re-locate you for Him to get you in the right place He destined for you to be.

The enemies are only able to see the whirlwind in your life, but they cannot see the end result of what the wind will give birth to. If you can stay focus in the place of prayer, the end result will be full of joy that eyes have not seen before nor ears heard of.

Whenever you feel the storm is too strong for you to bear, learn to position yourself in the right place, the flood will bring fruitful seed. The plan of the devil is for you to be frustrated, so that it would be hard for you to study the word of God. Holding on to God, is therefore a deliberate and conscious thing. Trusting Him will make you pray a prayer that will touch heaven.

When you are use to hold unto Him, you cannot act the way you feel any more, but the way God leads, you can no longer act carnally. Before you do any thing, you must first of all consult with God. He is the only one who has the ability to see beyond you.

Trusting Him may sometimes look stupid, but Abraham believed that God will provide another son for him, if He eventually made him slaughter Isaac. Though, what Abraham chose to do did not make sense.

In *Genesis 22:16b*, God says,
> *"for thou hast done this thing, and hast not withheld thy son , thine only son; That in blessing I will bless thee, and in multiplying, I will multiply thy seed as the stars of heaven, and the sand*

which is upon the seashore; and thy seed shall possess the gate of his enemies."

The choice which Abraham made a long time ago transferred the blessings to his generations till today. When you choose not to give up, God will help you to re route your journey of life.

> **Until your faith is tested and it passes the test, it cannot be regarded as faith.**

Holding on in the time of trouble is an act of faith.

Until your faith is tested and it passes, it cannot be regarded as faith. In the process of waiting, you must be able to repent genuinely of all your sins.

In the book of *Daniel 4*, King Nebukadenezar broke down and repented genuinely when the hands of God came upon him. He was away for a period of seven years, and God made sure that no one ascended his throne. God kept his throne for him, If God could do that for King Nebukadenezar, God can as well do which you can least expect. All He needs from you is a clean heart as you decide to hold on to Him. He will touch every area of your life that needs healing. Running a race and winning it is an individual decision.

There is always a lot of stops between where you

are, and where you are going. Each stop to your breakthrough has its individual package or challenge. At each stop, whatever experience you have is to build you up. You need the challenge to prepare you for you future. That which pushes you will determine your speed. Sometimes, when your life is too comfortable, you will not aspire and without any aspiration, life will be static.

For any mother to be successful, she must have a story to tell. If you are going through any form of storm, it is the plan of the devil to intimidate you so that you can give up.

The book of **Psalm 30:5b** which says that;
 " Weeping may endure for the night, but joy cometh in the morning,"

It encourages us that no matter how long ones problem may take, surely the day of solution will come. People have different nights. Your own weeping night may take one year, while the other person's night of weeping may take lesser time. But one thing that is sure is if you all depend on God , the morning of joy shall come.

A Mother's hope is in the assurance that the morning shall surely come for them to be celebrated. Though the waiting period is always very tough and full of struggles to survive, all you need to do is to stay put to be able to fight a good fight of faith.

When you are overwhelmed with sadness, faith in God will bring courage and smile back to your face. During trials, God wants to know how much of faith you have in Him. He wants to know how far you can trust and depend on Him.

Even if you have entered into a wrong ship like Jonah and you ended up in the belly of the fish, the moment you discover and change to trust on Him, He will make the fish to spit you out. He will create an escape route for you.

The Psalmist says ' in ***Psalm 121: 1***
> ***" I will lift up mine eyes unto the hills, from whence cometh my help"***

When you look down, there will be a bunch of issues for you to find; looking sides-ways, will bring dis-tractions; looking back will bring massive downfall. The only surviving place for you to look at, is up where your maker is. When you look up unto Him, you are doing that in a submissive way, He knows you are surrendering in totality. Our God who answereth by fire is duty bound to answer you.

The book of ***Proverb 24:16*** says:
> ***" Though a righteous man falls seven times, he rises again"***

This is to tell all mothers that those who are successful are those who do not choose to stay down when they fall. They are the mothers who pick up their pieces when they fall. They are not the mothers who are destabilized or get disturbed easily. Sometimes, life deals out a hand without any consideration of who you are or what you possess. Every child inherits life the way

The pain and agony inside of you which no one can see, feel, or cure could only be totally cured by trusting God alone.

he met it. No one has the ability to choose his or her mother.

There are many choices that are made on our behalf in life. This is why a mother needs to pray very hard for wisdom to direct the life of her child to the right direction. If you happen to have a child who is strong willed, you are not to give up on him.

Making a step towards God concerning the child will produce a great giant out of the child. A little step towards a right direction will always produce a great result .

During the period of waiting, you must be persistent in your prayer to eventually overcome the pain in your life. You must come to the realization of the fact that Jesus too had to overcome His pains and fears to attain His destiny through His experience at

Gethsemane.

Despite the beauty of the garden of Gethsemane, it was still a place of pressure and agony for Jesus. Jesus had people around Him, yet He was in pain. The pain and agony inside of you which no one can see, feel, or cure could only be totally cured by trusting God alone. Sometimes, what you are going through enables you to strive hard to get to your destiny. To reach your destiny, you have to keep holding on for the right season of God.

Is it your child that is giving you trouble? You must not give up on him, He is going to become the best child again if you continue to seek the face of God for the best direction concerning his life.

Submit everything concerning your child to the will of God. Do not submit to the will of the devil concerning your child. If you are the kind of a mother who had been saying; *" I can't handle this any more,"* I stand to correct you today that you need to beg God for forgiveness for that statement. It is the will of the devil to steal, kill and destroy your child, but it is for you to stand and say no to the plan of the devil. You have to let him know that he does not have any hold upon your child.

If you give up upon your child, then, you have given the devil the right to possess him. The devil's job is to set up mothers whose obedience are not fulfilled. If you are the mother who is still not spiritually strong to believe in the resurrection power of God, how will you be able to believe that such a power can touch your situation and give you eternal joy?

Once you believe in this power that rose Jesus from the dead, you will resist the devil, and you will be able to say ," no mater how long, I will wait." It is definitely the report of God that must reign supreme over your child. Use force to take your child back from the devil. The moment you submit to the will of God, He will determine your child's

Use force to take your child back from the devil. The moment you submit to the will of God, He will determine your child's destiny.

destiny. You cannot pray away the season of trials from your life, because as hard as Jesus prayed against going to the cross, He was still allowed to go by God for such a time as this for you and me.

After this season of wilderness in your life, believe that there is a land of milk and honey ahead of you if you do not give up.

During the moment of waiting, you need to be informative. You must equip yourself with knowledge. Ignorance is a deadly disease because it will create obstacles for you to grow so learn to look for new ideas to alleviate your pain.

The period of challenges, is not the time for you to think negative about life. It is the time for you to continue to hold to all God's promises concerning you. ***Psalm 42:1*** tells us about the way the deer longs for water, so you should continue to search for the living water of God to quench your thirst. You must continue to seek God.

When your victory is close, the battle is bound to get tougher, because there is a power struggle between you and your adversaries. This is the time for a woman who wants to be successful to continue to be unstoppable in the place of prayer. It is the time of reawakening.

It is the time to face the opposition with determination to win.
Every mother must be ready to turn her scars to stars. Your incidents must not become an altar of monument for you to continue to worship. You must not allow your past to prevent you from obtaining the plans of God for you.

Learn to imitate the right people during your waiting period. You must not join the multitude to do evil things, so learn to quit from every unwise association. The people you move with will surely rob on you either directly or indirectly.

Learn to move with people who plan to move up and

ahead.

Proverb 13:20 says,
> *" He that walketh with wise men shall be wise,*
> *but a companion of fools shall be destroyed"*

Learn to guard your tongue because unguarded tongue will make you sin. Whatever you say when in the wilderness determines how long you stay there. Your words can hold you in captivity and such can also tie you down permanently in the wilderness. Making negative confession will cause you to make several steps backward.

Using your eyes of understanding is very crucial in the time of waiting. Seeing well is the foundation of greatness. When your eyes of understanding are opened, you will be able to see the greatness ahead of you. Eyes that look are many, but the ones that see are very few. Seeing in this regard is having visions about what is ahead of you.

You should learn to pray for spiritual eyes to see what God has for you, because what you see is what you get. It is your vision that will dictate your action. When you are able to see clearly, you will be able to run your race on your own. Running another person's race will make you gasp for breath, and survival will not be easy. Allow the Lord to continue to be your shepherd until something happens.

Take your life really serious by not considering any offer from the world. Depending on God will give you great satisfaction. You will continue to be under His shadow for protection.

To any mother who chooses to be a survivor after being broken, all you need to do is not to give up ,nor quit but stay awake with the Lord, then you continue to push. If you get tired of the long waiting period, you will end up in the enemies' camp and you will waist away.

As you have chosen to wait on God, focusing on Him alone for every direction, your waiting can never be in vain.

You are the right candidate for God's kingdom. By focusing on God's directions for training of your children, you can never miss it. God will definitely reverse every irreversible for you and give you joy over your children in diverse ways.

He will definitely pay you back for all your days of trusting Him.

SING, O BARREN WOMAN

The book of *Isaiah 54:1* says:
> *"Sing, O barren, thou that didst not bear:*
> *break forth into singing, and cry aloud, Thou*
> *that didst not travail with a child,"*

Actually, this scripture is for the women who are lonely, neglected, not doing well, sad, childless, and also those whose children are not doing well, or difficult to raise.

Looking at the above scripture, how does it correlate

with the circumstances of the categories of people mentioned. It means that no matter the circumstance, you have every cause to sing your way into victory. Despite the challenges, God still say, they should sing for joy. No wonder, His thoughts differ from our own thoughts. For instance, an average human being's principle of being blessed is through hard work and serious savings, whereas, God's principle is sowing and reaping, that is, the more you give, the more you will be blessed.

The book of *Jeremiah 29:1*, says, the plans He has for everyone are the plans that will give us hope for our future. In the same chapter of the scripture , there are conditions that should be fulfilled by every woman who wants God's words to be a reality for her life. God does not want you to abandon or neglect His words, He wants His words to be light unto your dark areas of life. Therefore, He wants you to use your praise and worship to seek Him in the time of your trouble. He knows that in the place of your praise your long time chains will be broken and you will be set free.

Lucifer knows the importance of praise and worship to God. He knows how it works wonders before God, so he will do everything in his power to counter every motive behind people praising God. He was in charge of music in heaven before he was sent out with his demonic angels. Getting to the earth, he does not want

160

people to give honor to God in the place of worship. The devil understands all the benefits of praising God, therefore, praising God is a way of slapping the face of the devil. He hates the time of praise and worship with all his passion.

Praise is a sacrifice because it has to come from the heart. It is a weapon of spiritual warfare. It is an instrument of waging war with the kingdom of darkness because at the time of praise, you are telling the devil that he is loser. You are also making him to understand that no matter how long it takes you are not going to cross to his camp, and that you will wait for the most superior power to take over.

Does it still sound difficult to you mothers going through any ordeal in life? You have the right to say, Yes, it is. But the moment you burst into worshipping God in spirit and in truth, the devil is in trouble, because he knows he has lost the battle over you. At that stage, you will be claiming all that the devil has stolen from you. You are taking your joy, peace, dance, child, hope and every other thing back from the devil by force.

During your praise, you are delivering your spirit, soul and body from the kingdom of hell that owns loneliness, frustration, depression, failure, and childlessness.

You are also claiming your difficult child back from

the devil. You are rededicating your child into the hands of God Almighty. You are walking away from your messy past into the brighter future that God has for you.

When God commands you to sing to Him, He meant every bit of His words because the chaotic moment is going to be silent by force. The devil is always very timid and sad whenever the children of God are praising God. Doing this all the time is tearing down the kingdom of hell. It is a way of informing the devil that the battle over your life is over. It is also a way of telling him that the time of his discouragement is no longer in existence over that child that is proving difficult to raise.

God wants you to call those things that are not looking good to you as though they are already good. You can only live a supernatural life if His principles are followed step by step. He inhabits your praise. He gets happier with you when He sees you jumping for joy even in the midst of the trouble surrounding you. The encouragement puts His hands over your situation for immediate solution. Temptation and trials are real in life. To find a will of God for your life is a place of struggle.

No matter how bad your circumstance is ,you can still experience joy from God. For being the lifter of your head and the owner of your life, He deserves the praise and worship inside of you. The number of houses, diplomas, children, vehicles, and even money are not enough to give you joy because happiness is found outwardly, while joy is inwardly. Therefore, joy can only be found in Jesus alone. If you are grounded or rooted in any circumstance of life, it is only for a while. It shall soon be over if you can wait and begin to rejoice in it so that the devil will know that he has lost a battle over your life. In order to operate with God, you have to cooperate with the holy spirit for direction.

To heal your broken heart and give you beauty for all your ashes, you have to get rid of your bitterness, negativism, bad thought, malice, shame, hurt, and most importantly, learn to allow the joy of the Lord to be your strength to sail through.

> **If you are grounded or rooted in any circumstance of life, it is only for a while. It shall soon be over if you can wait.**

Joy does not come in the place of weeping, but in the place of praising God for what He has done and what He will continue to do. Joy does not come when you feel guilty or blame yourself.

You cannot rejoice when you look down on yourself. Your circumstances will change when you release yourself of all bad thoughts and start to rejoice in the place of praise. The moment you stop to magnify your circumstances above God, He will begin to move in that circumstance.

Do you want to live a powerful life? Learn to make a joyful noise to the Lord, by coming to His presence with singing. Complaining is way of discouraging oneself, but being thankful is a way of remembering God's faithfulness to you.

Isaiah 61:7 says ,
" For your shame ye shall have double; and for confusion they shall rejoice in their portion; therefore in their land they shall possess the double; everlasting joy shall be unto them. "

This is another great promise of God for mothers that are going through any form of set back , God said , He is going to give you double for your trouble. To obtain the promises of God, you cannot overload yourself with sadness and broken heart. You have to step into the atmosphere of worship, whereby God , will also be pleased in you.

For a childless woman, delay is a denial. God does not forget any of His creature. The fact that a friend has children before you does not stop your own when God is ready to answer you.

Are you aware of the fact that no one ever heard of

164

Peninnah's children, nor even their names? But, Hannah started child bearing late, and God gave her Samuel who was a unique child and a prophet in Israel. God has already known the end from the beginning. Therefore, your action and attitude matter to God during your waiting period.

WHY WE NEED TO SING DURING TRIALS:

In the world that we are today, it may look like there is not much to make you happy , but the grace of sleeping and waking up is enough to thank God for. You must learn to rejoice on purpose, in order to put the devil to shame.

Nehemiah 8:10 says
"The joy of the Lord is your strength".

It is in the presence of God that you can be charged. Singing closes the mouth of the devil concerning any circumstance. As you sing praises to God, He changes your sorrowful garment to the garment of joy and peace. Singing is a sacrifice to God. Sacrifice of praise is the fruit of our lips.

The book of *Hebrews 13:15*, says,
"by therefore, let us offer the sacrifice of praise to God continually, that is, the fruit of our lips giving thanks to His names".

God wants our lips to be new everyday to give thankful praises to Him. He enjoys being praised for all He had done, and what He will continue to do.

Praising God brings revelation by creating awareness into the realms of the spirit. It makes you have an insight into the things of the spirit. In the place of praise, angels come ascending and descending rejoicing with you.

David was a singer, dancer, and a rejoicer. He constantly spoke of God's faithfulness and goodness in the place of worship. When David praised the Lord, he did it with all his strength and soul.

The book of *Psalm 103 : 1* says,
"Bless the Lord, O my soul; and all that is within me, bless His holy name". No wonder, God called David, a man after His own heart".

David knew how to appease God with his praise and worship all the time.

In the process of praising God, He makes sure you do not lack any good thing. He makes a way for you where there was no way. Praising God makes Him go out of His way to grant you favor because He does not want you to become a laughing stock. He knows that the devil is waiting for you to backslide, therefore, God will get out of His way to meet your heartfelt need.

In the process of worshipping Him, He will open up your womb for conception. That long time barrenness will become a story. He knows your dependability is on Him, He will not put you to shame. As you praise Him, His everlasting kindness will have mercy on you, and do that which no one can do.

In the book of *Isaiah 51:12*, God said, He is the one that can comfort you, and that you should not be afraid of a man that shall die.

Devil does not have a way of comforting any one, instead, he takes joy in compiling problem. It is only in God's presence that you can be established and be far from oppression, fear and terror.

Praising God brings revelation; you will sense the spirit of God around you and you will become sensitive, seeing into the realm of the spirit.

As you continue to worship the Lord, whoever plans to gather against you for you to remain barren, shall surely fall for your sake.

In the place of worship, there is no weapon that is formed against you that can prosper. The way God opened the wombs of Hannah, Elizabeth, Sarah and Rachael, yours too shall be opened, and you shall

167

become a mother of the heavenly sent children. God said, that as you praise Him, every mountain ahead of you shall depart, every hill shall be removed, but that His kindness shall never depart from you, neither shall the covenant of His peace be removed from you.

Praising Him will make Him to become your shepherd at all time. He will prepare multiples of food before you, and He will make your enemies watch you as you eat. He will anoint you and make you overflow with blessings.

Praises makes God to become your light. He will order your steps and uphold you with His hands. He gives you visions as to what is ahead of you. He plans with you so that you do not get out of His boundary. Fear will totally vanish, because you will be strong, courageous and full of energy to do exploits.

Praises makes you to trust nothing else than the name of God. It builds up your confidence that He can do anything. His name alone will be on your lips. Your deliverance is sure because sickness will not have a choice than to fade away in its secret place.

The book of *Psalm 48:1-2,* says,
" Great is the Lord, and greatly to be praised in the city of our Lord, in the mountain of His holiness. Beautiful for situation, the joy of the whole earth, is mount Zion, on the sides of the north, the city of the great King".

This scripture is another big confirmation of how God enjoys your praise and worship. He said, He is going to appear beautiful in that situation that is weighing you down. Can you imagine how the ugly situation will look like when Jesus appears in His beauty to put His own sweetness on the bitter life?

His awesomeness is the expectation of all that wait upon Him during the moment of struggles. He is great and mighty in power to be the greatest physician to heal every long standing disease. He is the only one we can give all our praises to, and He will never share it with anybody.

In conclusion, the book of **Romans 3:4** says:
   "Let God be true, but every man a liar; "

This statement brings confidence that no man can give, except God. Whatever He says, He will do, is what He will do speedily. We should not be like the unbelievers who do not have hope or faith, we should hold on firmly to all His promises to come to reality in our lives.

At all times, keep praising Him for what He has done and for what He will do, He will never put you to shame.

MAKING A NECESSARY SHIFT.

It is required of every Godly mother to make a necessary shift to a higher level of attainment of her destiny as ordained by God. It is time for you to allow God to be the foundation of your birth, marriage, and health so that you can come out of where you have been caged for so long and align with your original destiny by divine arrangement.

God is going to take you to your place of possession; He is taking you to a place you can call your own.

There will be a shaking that will begin to lift you up to that right place where anything that is holding your blessings will begin to release and return all that they stole from you.

Joseph did not start well, but he ended well. All that the enemies planned for evil for him was the raw material that God used to take him to his divine destiny. Have they said that nothing good can come out of your life and that of your children? If they wait long enough, they will see the hands of God in your life. This is your season of

You should be aware of the fact that you have a choice as to what you want for your life and that of your children, hence, it is time for you to handle your life according to how you value it.

returning to your lost glory. Those who have rejected you will begin to seek you.

The book of *Jeremiah 29:28* already made it clear that God's plans for you are of good and not of evil. The promises of God are your legitimate right which you need to acquire by all means. The only barrier that can stand against you is only you. God is interested in your well - being. It is time for you to get tired of eating leftover with your children, therefore, you need all the energy in you to aspire to make every necessary shift to a higher level. God did not create His children to wallow in abject poverty, He is interested in seeing His glory all over you. Crumbs are only for dogs and goats to eat, not for any one who knows her right as a child of God.

You are not to eat the crumbs that fall from the table of the wicked. The time of playing the under-dog kind of a life is no more. This is a wake - up call for all mothers, where ignorance should no longer be an excuse.

You should be aware of the fact that you have a choice as to what you want for your life and that of your children, hence, it is time for you to handle your life according to its value to you. It is therefore time for you to make a decision not allow the devil to rob you of what belongs to you. You will then choose to rise up with every aggression in you to force a change with the sword of the spirit that God placed in your hands.

As a mother, you cannot afford to be lazy to play your God given role spiritually, emotionally, physically, and domestically over your children? You need to get serious and be more assertive, because nothing good comes easy. You need to fight a good fight of faith. Attainment of your destiny involves your active participation and obedience to God's directives. God is not going to do anything if you claim to be satisfied with your position and that of your children. But, if you are fed up of your present condition, the urge inside of you will push you to determine to seek help from the Lord.

If you put your vehicle gear to a level one, there is a maximum speed limit the vehicle can go for it to start giving you a signal for a change in the gear level. The faster you want your vehicle to go, the higher the gear level. When the gear is at the highest level, definitely, the acceleration of the vehicle will correlate with the level of the gear. This is exactly the way you have to change your speed in the things of your life if you desire to make a necessary shift to be a person that God designed you to be. If you do not move fast to work towards achieving your goals in life, the devil will kill your vision.

Once you follow God's instructions, it will be easy for you to make every necessary change that you need. The enemy cannot stop the Lord from setting a table before you, but if you do not follow God's instruction and principles, the enemy can stop you from sitting at the table to enjoy the good food. The enemy can make you sit under the table to eat crumbs. This is why you constantly need to stay under God's obedience.

The book of *1Chronicles 4:9-10* narrated the story of Jabez as a sorrowful child. The sight of Jabez always

174

reminded the mother of the sorrow and pain that surrounded his birth. Jabez did not just change his name,
but he had a clear understanding of how the name was
working against his destiny. Nobody heard anything
about his father. The father must have abandoned him
with the mother because of the sorrowful memory
that the boy kept bringing to them. He might not want
to be associated with him at all, but the mother will
always remain the mother to his child no matter how
bad the situation is. One day, Jabez looked round and
found that every thing was against him so he turned to
God who had the ability to change any situation He
knew it was the will of God for him to prosper; he
knew God was a good God. He prayed to God to bless
him, to enlarge his coast, that His hand should be with
him, and he should be kept from evil.

Jabez must have known God to be a covenant keeping
God. He invaded his situation with prayer of faith. He
used aggressiveness to pray by tapping into all the
blessings of Abraham and used it to pray to God. He
rejected his status-quo of no more crumbs. He sent it
backwards to the devil, by turning every curse in his
life to blessing. He reversed every curse spoken into
his life. He refused to look unto anybody for solution,
but unto God.

If you as a woman seem satisfied with your present
condition, then it will be like that forever or even get
worse. When you talk to God to remember the

covenant He had for Abraham, concerning your situation, every limitation will be removed. This is in obedience to His word that He would never say anything without fulfilling it.

Abraham obeyed God and enjoyed the reward. Job, in the midst of his pain did not reject God. He said, "even though, you slay me, yet will I follow". He chose to obey and hold on to His words, he found favor and all that he lost was restored to him in multiple ways.

Ruth is another example of a person who had her limitations removed, because she surrendered to the will of God; God entered into partnership with her by directing her path and leading her to where she met with her miracle. She did not allow the flesh to rule her, her Godly attitude made her to enter into the lineage of Jesus .

To be able to make a quick shift to a higher level, you need the right association with the ability to dream big. Unwise association will keep you waiting in the land of Egypt.

The book of **Proverbs 13:20** says that whoever walks with wise men shall be wise. Who are the people you spend your leisure time with? Whoever you associate with will definitely influence your thinking. If you move with negative thinkers, you will never be able

176

think positively. If your friends do not believe in stepping into the deep waters with God, you will lose your faith in God, and you will never achieve anything positive. You should be selective as to who you spend your time with. A lot of good people have been destroyed by ungodly friends. When you move with people who mock the name of the Lord, or the gospel of our Lord Jesus Christ, definitely you will be affected by such acts.

If Ruth took counsel from an unwise person, she would have missed her destiny in life. Ahab was counseled by Jezebel and it led to his destruction. Unwise association will definitely pull you down.

As a mother who wants to make a meaningful shift from eating crumbs to sitting at the table that is set by God with varieties of delicacies, like righteousness, joy in the holy ghost, peace, healing, deliverance, salvation, and blessings :

* You need to be born anew.
* You need to obey every instruction given by God.
* You must not move with unwise association.
* You must get to the level of outright submission to God.
* You must understand God's principles.
* You must adhere to His words.
* You must be ready to pass the test of time.

*   Your total dependence must be on Him only.
*   You will be far from Unforgiveness and bitterness.

As you strive to align yourself to the above principles, God will grant you all the covenants He had for Abraham, Isaac, and Jacob. All your expectations shall definitely produce good results in Jesus name.

Amen.

CONCLUSION

Looking back to that little girl of more than six decades ago, from a humble and notable background, now a mother and even a grand mother, serving the Lord with all her heart and her might, it could only be God!!!

Looking back to where she was coming from, to where she is now; marching on with full acceleration from amidst the thorns; one can say with a lot of emphasis that it could only have been God. Did God ever promise it would be easy? No, is the answer. As she keeps running fast with the talents God gave her, fear is unable to freeze her. Her battles do not need to speak, but her victory tells it all. With God on her side , she changed the values of what life handed to her and started all over again, bouncing back with full determination to succeed at all cost. What a good God she continues to serve.

Thank God for the womb that carried this little girl, thank God for the safe delivery of the little bouncing baby girl, though, a bit tough according to history by the eldest brother. Thank God for the nurturing she received from her mother while growing up and thank God for the existing love that surrounded her growth. As she was growing, she was nurtured to be coura-geous, full of energy, and strength to face any situation that comes her way. Her mother, by name Dorcas who is now of blessed memory nurtured her in the way of the Lord very early in life. Though Dorcas did not come from a Christian background, it was her decision before the birth of her baby girl to serve God, hence, she was baptized by immersion, and she was given a baptismal name as Dorcas. Since then, she vowed never to serve any other god, but Jehovah God. Dorcas would never miss the early morning prayer in the church and every Sunday service. The little girl grew up following her mother to church.

As a teenager, she was in the church choir, learning how to sing and praise the Lord. By the mother's understanding of the teaching she received during the baptismal class, she vowed to live her life like the "Dorcas" of the bible. Giving to the needy became a thing of joy to her. Even in the midst of nothing, she would give whatever she was able to get to the needy around her most especially to the men of God. You know, the little girl wondered why the mother kept doing this.

Another thing the little girl learned as she was growing was how to hold on to the truth on any situation and never look back to accept the lie of the devil. Dorcas taught her little girl to pray, and that no matter how long it takes for one to continue to lie, truth will always reign; and that the truth will eventually bring freedom. The little girl held on to this fact about life

180

and continued to live by it. As a young girl, she kept watching her mom as she played a leadership role in the family, church and even in the community. No wonder the little girl grew up to sail the boat of leadership with ease as she graduated top of her class in high school. She served as the Senior Prefect in high school, a position in which she successfully led about five hundred students without any crisis or conflict.

The little girl grew to be a matured young adult to make her decisions and choices by herself. Even when she did not know what it meant to accept Christ, she believed in God, and the little she had understanding in His words.

She kept going to church and prayed according to the level of her understanding. Based upon all she was thought while growing up by her mother, she became strong and energetic to face life with courage and the little she knew in the Lord 's Prayer and *Psalm 23*. This may sound funny, but for a long time, all she depended on was how to recite the Lord 's Prayer and Psalm 23 and little words of prayer. Some of the decisions made at that time might have been blindly made without knowing the consequence.

Before mother Dorcas went to be with the Lord, she laid a good foundation for her little girl to build upon when tribulations came. She left an indelible mark amongst her family, church, and in her community till date.

Somewhere along the way, in the midst of confusion, God caught the attention of the little girl by all means. When I say, '*by all means*', I mean every word of it. When storm came, she had no alternative other than to keep remembering the valuable words of her mom based on truth, hard work, staying focused, and serving no other god. She chose to cling to God by all means. Who knows? Probably, for such a time as this, so that she can fulfill the purpose of God for her life.

The foundation laid by mother Dorcas for her little girl became her bedrock today. The foundation was based on God as the all in all. The little girl continued to grow in age, knowledge and wisdom of God.

Going back to the basic foundation of what mother Dorcas showed her was not difficult for her. Turning back to the Lord when trials came was not difficult; it was not a questionable option. Therefore, serving the Lord became her priority. Her focus became how to grow in the Lord through the knowledge of His words. She became thirsty for the word of God.

Wise association was an incentive for the girl when trials came which is why she made sure that she was not surrounded by devilish counselors. Along her journey in the wilderness, God ordered her steps to a right place of worship, and under a truthful shepherd with undiluted and non compromising teaching. She was surrounded by the right co-workers, family members and right friends who were all of tremendous help, It could only have been God who knows the end from the beginning. As a young adult, her mom talked to her about every thing; she never left anything unsaid. She was fond of talking, but mainly sensible talk. She talked about her hard and pleasant life experiences, most of the time in parables. Among her business associates, she was highly respected for her immense contribution at any given time. Without any coaxing, her intelligent quotient was very high. She left no stone untouched in the family. She was a mother in a million.

Modern day mothers, what do you talk about to your child? What lessons are you giving to them? Don't think they are not watching or listening to you. What do you expect your child to say about you? Do not plant wickedness into the heart of your child. Do not hand over the spirit of unforgiveness to your child. If you have been badly hurt, let your maker be the right judge and not you nor your child. Allow your child to have a good memory of you. God's plans towards us are good, but we have to do our own part to bring the plans to realization.

The book of *Jeremiah 29:11,* says
> *"For I know the thought that I have towards you,*
> *saith the Lord;*
> *Thoughts of peace and not of evil,*
> *to give you an expected end".*

The knowledge of this scripture always gives me joy and inner peace. It makes me know that nothing catches God unawares about me. He knows the end from the beginning. No wonder this season has come for the little seed that mother Dorcas planted and watered so hard to germinate to a full grown woman of over six decades in years today
.

In between the growth of the seed to a full fruit, there were various winds, but the foundations laid by Dorcas in terms of prayers, courage, faith, giving, and the other legacy protected the life of this baby girl from being carried away by the wind.

Over six decades later, here I am now rejoicing in the presence of God, from that bouncing baby girl to a woman of God. All his plans for me are all of good and never of any evil.

As a mother what do you want the world to remember you for? Even, while alive, what foundation are you laying for your children and people that know you? Do you realize that your life is even a gift for you? What are you doing with the children that God gave you? Do you realize that you cannot handle them anyhow?

You need to know that you are going to be accountable for the kind of training you gave your children. To do a good job on your children, you need to go back to the basic foundation of God's principles. Nothing can be achieved without His help because a life without Christ will lead to crisis. You have to let your child know the importance of making heaven, so that you can both meet again. If you alone make it to heaven and your child does not, you as a mother have missed it. Every Godly parent must learn a big lesson from the way Priest Eli paid for how he handled his children with levity. As a servant of God, do not be pre-occupied at the expense of your biological children.

The suggestion of Jethro in the bible is a good one which may be of help to you, so that , you do not overlook that vital aspect also. A word is enough for the wise.

I am grateful to God for the salvation of my soul. He bought me with a costly price and delivered me from the den of lions and the physical fiery furnace prepared for me by my enemies. How many can I count? He molded me to His satisfaction and gave me a turn around life for good; He is worthy of my praise.

When pain came my way, it did not break me, instead, it built me up to who I am today for such a time as this. God's mercy defined who I am and therefore I refuse to let any thing change it. Overcoming every storm through the mercy of God puts abundant praise to my mouth now. I have never seen this kind of a merciful father who used His blood to cleanse me and change my life. He used all within His power to catch my attention for this kind of a moment. Who knows, may be somebody like me might have wandered away if not by His mercy.

To the readers of this remarkable book most especially mothers, God did not say you will not have challenges, but He also promised that He will not give you more than what you can handle if you walk in His purpose. He has the record of everything that you are doing. You cannot hide from Him, if you cover up, He can still fish you out. He knows every strand of hair on your head, so He is the only one who can use your problem to build you up to fulfill His will in your life, if you can only depend on Him.

For you to be called the Ultimate, Unique, and Remarkable Mom by your children, you should be willing to go back to the biblical principles as set up by God.

My mother, Mrs. Dorcas Oluborode (Nee Ajayi-Oromu) gave me a legacy that has helped my life in every aspect of life, mostly in Christ, and I in turn have been able to share this legacy with my four daughters who are now all Godly mothers serving the Lord Jesus Christ. I know that the generations to come will have a great legacy to live by and I hope that reading this book, will also inspire and encourage you to do the same. ***God Bless you.***

About the Author

Julie Olamide Ariyo

She has been a teacher for almost three decades. She also has a gift of teaching which she has been using in the kingdom of God and is available to speak at women's conferences for em-powerment.

Teaching to her is a noble and rewarding profession and it continues to give her the utmost joy. Imparting knowledge into the lives of today's professionals and even servants of God is something she continues to naturally enjoy. Above all, she does not trade the valuable and magnificent role that God gave her as a mother for anything.

She is a mother of four beautiful women and blessed with several grandchildren. She loves being every-thing it takes to be a woman of honor and integrity.

She has a Bachelors degree in Economics from City College of New York and a Masters degree in

Guidance Counseling from the University of Arizona. U.S.A

Presently, she is Teaching in one of Maryland schools and also an Elder in the Redeemed Christian Church of God , Jesus House D.C. USA.

She is a non compromising woman of God who does not believe in settling for less in every aspect of life and she believes the sky is the beginning of her life achievement.